PICK YOUR BRAINS
about
FRANCE

Marian Pashley

Illustrations by
Caspar Williams & Craig Dixon

CADOGAN

Acknowledgements
The author and publisher would like to thank
'guest editor' James (aged 12).

Thanks to Natalie Pomier for all her help.

Published by Cadogan Guides 2004
Reprinted 2004
Copyright © Marian Pashley 2004

Illustrations by Caspar Williams and Craig Dixon
Illustrations and map copyright © Cadogan Guides 2004
Map by (TW)

Cadogan Guides
Network House, 1 Ariel Way, London W12 7SL
info@cadoganguides.co.uk
www.cadoganguides.com

The Globe Pequot Press
246 Goose Lane, PO Box 480, Guilford,
Connecticut 06437–0480

Design and typesetting by Mathew Lyons
Printed in Italy by Legoprint

A catalogue record for this book is available
from the British Library
ISBN 1-86011-155-6

Contents

Map   4

Vital Facts and Figures   5

French History in a Nutshell   11

Local Customs: How the French Live   23

A School Day in France   39

Fabulous Buildings and Sights   45

Great Inventors, Famous Artists,
Scientists and a Soldier   61

A Spoonful of French Music   75

Food and Drink   81

Festivals and National Celebrations   89

Markets   97

A Little Bit of Sport   101

Odds and Ends   109

Emergency Phrases   119

Good Books and Wicked Websites   125

Quirks and Scribbles   128

Not to scale!

Vital Facts
and Figures

Area: France measures about 211,000 square miles (547,000 square km), making it the largest country in Europe, but not the world. Britain measures 95,000 square miles (245, 000 square km), so France is about 2.2 times the size.

Population: France has a population of something over 60 million people – just a little bit more than Britain.

Capital: Paris (but of course you already knew that, didn't you?). But in Roman times the main city was Lyon.

Other major cities include: Lyon, Lille, Marseille, Toulouse, Bordeaux, Nantes.

Currency: the euro.
The French franc, which was replaced by the euro in 2002, dated back to the 14th century. It was introduced in an effort to stabilize the economy in the chaotic times of the Hundred Years' War.

Internet domain: fr.

Time difference: one hour ahead of the UK.

Shares a border with: eight other countries: Spain, Monaco and Andorra on the south side, Italy, Germany and Switzerland to the east, and Belgium and Luxembourg to the north.

Its biggest island is Corsica, in the Mediterranean Sea.

Coastline: the French coastline is famously spectacular and varied, with glorious sandy beaches in certain regions and dramatic rocky cliffs and shingle in others. As well as the

Mediterranean it is surrounded by the Atlantic Ocean and the English Channel.

Biggest mountain: Mont Blanc, in the French Alps, at 15,771ft (4,807m).

Languages and regions: The official language is French, but there are dialects spoken in some regions: Provençal, Breton, Flemish, Basque, Catalan, Corsican and Alsatian (but these languages are generally used very little).

Climate: France can be very hot in the summer months, particularly in the south/southwest. In Paris and central France it can range from scorching in summer or temperate in spring and autumn to freezing during the winter. But it rains a great deal less than in England. The Mistral, which you may hear about, is an infamous strong southwesterly wind, which can cause a lot of damage when it blows!

The Channel Tunnel: This may be how you will travel from Britain to France, through a tunnel built under the English Channel that allows trains to travel under the sea. You can either travel by Eurostar train, or sit in your car on board the Shuttle, a car-carrying train.

The Channel Tunnel is an idea that has been talked and dreamt about for centuries. But it was finally finished in 1994 (two years later than planned), and was fraught with problems and technical hitches. France and Britain went about it by each tunnelling from their respective sides – from Sangatte in France and from

METROPOLITAIN

Folkestone in England, to meet up somewhere in between. The French managed to complete their side first, much to the embarrassment of the British. Everyone was mighty relieved when the tunnel met in the middle!

Driving: Many French love their cars, and you will see a great many Renaults, Citroëns and Peugeots, which are made in France and exported all over the world. The minimum age to drive a car is 18.

Toll roads: Many of France's motorways are 'toll roads', which are roads that you have to pay to travel along. The upside is that they get you there much quicker and more directly. On some you get a ticket and have to pay at the end of the motorway, on others you pay several times along the way at barriers. Expect your driver to frequently whinge about how much it costs! If you have the correct money you simply throw it into a type of metal basket by the side of the tollbooth. This is the fun bit and should definitely be tried if your hot, cross driver will let you. The machines are very sensitive and weigh the money, so they know

8

if the wrong coins (or something that is not even a coin!) are thrown in, in which case the barriers will stay firmly locked down.

The Métro, Paris: This underground railway system first ran in 1898 and now has 322 stations. The entrances to many stations are beautifully elaborate and old-fashioned, and then once inside, the trains and platforms seem surprisingly modern in contrast. The trains run from about 5.30am to 1.00am. You can get a multi-purpose ticket, called a *Carte Orange* (orange card) that allows you on buses and overground trains as well. You can buy single tickets, that are a fixed price per journey, whatever the distance, or you can buy a *carnet* – ten tickets at once for a discount price.

RER: This is a special super-fast underground and overground system that links the suburbs of Paris to the centre of the city.

Buses: Major towns and cities in France have very good bus systems, and some also have trams, that nip around quickly on their own tracks through the city streets.

Trains: One of the best ways to travel around France is by train. The tracks extend out to all areas of the country, and are state-run by the SNCF (standing for *Société Nationale des Chemins de Fer Français* – meaning the National French Railway Company). The trains run very well and pretty

much on time, and are a quite cheap way to travel.

TGV: You might get to travel on one of these super-fast trains, if you are very lucky. TGV stands for *'train à grande vitesse'*, which means 'train of great speed', and they really are. You only get them for the longer journeys through France.

So how fast is super-fast? These trains reach speeds of up to 560kph (350mph), which when you compare it to the fastest you are likely to have travelled in a car (around 130kph or 80mph) is seriously quick. It won't be something you forget in a hurry. All the French countryside whizzing past in such a blur makes ordinary trains seem like Victorian horse-drawn stage-coaches in comparison.

Children from four to eleven travel half-price, but if a dog weighs over 6kg it has to be bought a half-price ticket!

French
History in
a Nutshell

France has had a very eventful history. It hasn't always been the same size and shape as it is today, and has been invaded by many different peoples. It is now a vast country with a very interesting and rich culture, but that hasn't happened without a lot of wars – with other countries as well as among its own people.

Prehistoric people first set foot in France about a million years ago and they hunted bison and reindeer, and lived in caves. It took thousands of years for these Stone Age people to develop the sort of life we might just recognize today,

---

You can see Prehistoric France in:

☞ Lascaux, The Dordogne, southwest France, where the Lascaux caves contain the most famous cave paintings in the world (they're not open to the public, because people's breath can damage the paintings, but you can see brilliant replicas next door at Lascaux II).

☞ Carnac in Brittany, where 3,000 ancient rocks arranged in mysterious lines and patterns have puzzled archaeologists for many years. Were they used for religious worship, for funerals or as ancient calendars, using the sun and moon to mark out time? No one knows.

☞ Nîmes, in the south of France, where there is a magnificent 20,000-seater Roman amphitheatre called *Les Arènes*. Built for massive entertainments such as gladiator fights and military displays, it is still used for concerts and sporting events. There are several other Roman monuments in the town, and another amphitheatre nearby in Arles.

☞ Pont du Gard, not that far from Nîmes. This is an amazing Roman aqueduct that carried water high over a river valley. It was built in 19 BC and was in use for a thousand years.

☞ Alise-Ste-Reine in Burgundy where, on a hill called *Mont Auxois*, there is a statue of Julius Caesar's greatest opponent, a chieftain called Vercingétorix. His refusal to be defeated by the Romans inspired the famous cartoon character Astérix.

where they grew crops, kept animals, made tools and followed a religion.

By 600 BC, many different tribes of people had come to live in France and some, like the Celts and the Greeks, ruled parts of the country. The Romans were the most powerful and by 52 BC, after many battles, the Roman emperor Julius Caesar declared a victory. The Romans stayed for several hundred years and brought many ideas from back home – heating, hot baths, good roads – and introduced Latin from which the French language would eventually develop. And (what a cheek!) they renamed their newly conquered territory and called it Gaul, and made Lyon the main city.

Roman rule had ended by the fifth century AD and for the first time in hundreds of years, France was in a little bit

of a mess! Tribes from Germany invaded the country and
one of them, called the Franks, became extremely powerful.
They introduced Christianity to the people, made Paris their
capital and gave the country the name 'Francia' (nearly
'France' but not quite…) There was always something
strange about this tribe, not least the curious fact that when
they buried their kings, they put into the grave large
numbers of tiny golden bees. Nobody knows why.

It seems to have been difficult for anyone to hold on to
power in France, and before long rival lords, kings and even
Vikings were fighting it out to be the new rulers. It was many
hundreds of years before the country settled down. When it
did, in the Middle Ages, France had become prosperous and
very religious. Magnificent abbeys and cathedrals were built,
and monks played a great part in encouraging the spread of
reading and writing. The country was growing stronger
thanks to the efforts of knights, crusaders and scholars, and
France even conquered England in 1066.

By now, France was one of the most powerful countries in Europe but even so, in 1328, it found itself at war again, this time in the Hundred Years' War with the English (yes, it really did last just over a hundred years!). The legendary Joan of Arc, a shepherd girl turned soldier, helped the French to win this war. And then just as the French people were thinking 'Hooray, time for a bit of peace and quiet, to grow some food, and spend time with my family', another war broke out. This time, they were fighting among themselves about religion and (what a surprise!) about who was going to rule the country.

Surprisingly, despite everything, the royal palaces and the

15

noblemen's
houses became the
flashiest in Europe.
There was at last a
strong monarchy and the king,
François I, fell in love with all things Italian – Italian art,
music, architecture, cooking and fashion. He even asked the
great Italian painter and inventor Leonardo da Vinci to visit
France. This period is called the Renaissance, which means
'rebirth' and refers to the fact that people were beginning to
think less about religion and more about new subjects such as

---

You can see Renaissance and Grand Siècle France in:

☞ Château de Chenonceau in the Loire Valley, one of
the loveliest and most visited castles in the whole
country. No expense was spared: it was partly built
over a river, it showed off expensive Italian features
and one of its fountains spouted wine!

☞ Versailles (near Paris), where life in this magnificent
royal palace was the height of luxury. King Louis XIV
built Versailles, and its design and decoration
influenced all of Europe. Visit the Queen's bedroom,
where the queen had to give birth in public!

science and poetry, which didn't refer to God.

France remained at peace and so all this sophistication and learning was able to continue, and by the beginning of the 17th century, the country was more dazzling than ever and the King, Louis XIV (that stands for 'Louis the 14th'), had immense power. People refer to this time as the 'Grand Siècle', meaning 'the Great Age'. People such as Racine and Molière were writing some of the most famous French plays at this time, and mathematicians and philosophers were producing great theories about the world which everyone argued about. And while all this important thinking was going on, a writer called Charles Perrault was dreaming up lovely fairy tales such as Sleeping Beauty, Cinderella and Little Red Riding Hood.

For royalty and noblemen, life in France at this time was probably good fun. But as you can imagine, all the centuries of war had actually made France quite poor and the rich were doing their best to ignore this fact. Soldiers had to be paid and the towns and villages which had been destroyed had to be rebuilt. To pay for past wars, and for the future wars of the next three kings (all called Louis), a portion of money, or tax, was demanded from every citizen. Considering that many people were already very poor, this was very unpopular!

At the same time as they

17

You can see Revolutionary and Napoleonic France in:

☞ the Conciergerie in Paris, where prisoners, including Queen Marie-Antoinette, were locked in cells, awaiting the guillotine.

☞ the Eglise du Dôme inside the Hôtel des Invalides in Paris, where Napoleon is buried in the crypt in six coffins, each one fitting inside the other. The decoration of the tomb is extremely lavish.

☞ And everywhere you see the French flag (called the *Tricolore*), you can think of the Revolution because this was the flag they used, the first time that the red, white and blue appeared together.

were paying this tax, the people of France saw the upper classes living a life of luxury. They only had to go to Versailles to see how the other half lived! The end result was the French Revolution of 1789, which started in Paris when angry crowds attacked the prison called the Bastille. The rich and powerful became extremely worried – would they be attacked next? The King (Louis XVI) and Queen (Marie-Antoinette) and many others fled for their lives, but were caught and beheaded by guillotine. A machine made especially for chopping people's heads off, the guillotine might make you rightly think it's the stuff of nightmares, but it was actually invented in order to be less cruel. The logic was that once the blade fell, at least it would all be over quickly!

So, France was now no longer ruled by a royal family but by the leaders of the Revolution and then by the famous military general, Napoleon Bonaparte, who made himself emperor in 1804. Being a soldier, Napoleon wanted to go to war and conquer other countries, and so he invaded Spain, Italy, Germany and even Russia, until he was defeated by

Britain and Prussia at the Battle of Waterloo, in Belgium. But he wasn't just interested in war; he had supported the Revolution and wanted to do something for the French people. So he set up a new school system, a national bank and he encouraged modern ideas and inventions.

After Napoleon's death, there was more squabbling over who was going to run France and for a little while there was a king again but not for very long. Confusing, isn't it? It must have been for everyone – one minute you've got a king, the next an emperor. But, as has happened before in French history, the people just got on with things and by the end of the 19th century, it was an exciting time to be living in France. This period was known as the 'Belle Époque' which means the 'beautiful era'. New writers and artists, including the Impressionist painters such as Monet and Renoir, were on the scene, cars and bicycles were thrilling inventions, Louis Blériot became the first person to fly across the Channel in a little plane in 1909 and the early days of cinema captured everyone's imagination.

Thank goodness France was able to have a few decades of peace and quiet and fun because bad times were just around the corner. In 1914, war with Germany was declared and the First World War had begun. This terrible war killed 1.3 million French soldiers, and wrecked much of northern France where most of the war was fought.

When the war ended in 1918, the country rallied round and tried to enjoy itself again, and Paris became a very fashionable city where everyone wanted to live. However, by the end of the 1930s, if you had anywhere else to go then it was best to leave Paris because the Second World War had started, and France as well as Britain was at war with Germany. The Germans invaded France. Many French people formed a group called the Resistance and they tried to overthrow the Germans by bombing railway lines, spying

☞ Paris, where some entrance signs to the *Métro* are designed in the Art Nouveau style which was very popular during the *Belle Époque*. The letters have wavy lines and are very flowery, and you'll recognize the same style in many posters and drawings from that time.

☞ Verdun in northern France, where many First World War battles were fought. The fighting here was so fierce that entire villages were destroyed and you can see huge areas of land covered with craters from hundreds of shells being dropped. There is an underground fort nearby where many soldiers would stay until the shelling had stopped.

and just generally trying to interfere with Nazi rule. The Resistance performed many dangerous acts, and you can see many monuments to their bravery all over France.

Paris was finally freed from Nazi rule in 1944 and by the time the war had ended in 1945 had suffered great damage. Buildings, roads and factories had been destroyed and it was a long struggle before the country recovered. From 1958, France was run by General de Gaulle (the President) but his government liked to control things too much and found it difficult to listen to the people when they wanted things to change. In 1968, large numbers of students and nine million workers led a protest in Paris, and eventually de Gaulle lost power, to be replaced by a new President.

The France you see today is a prosperous country. It's hard to believe it has gone through so much turmoil but if you are there on Bastille Day (14 July, when the French noisily celebrate the Revolution) or if your parents or

grandparents remember the Second World War or the time in 1968 when there was nearly another revolution, then you'll be reminded of how quickly things can change in France!

Local Customs: How the French Live

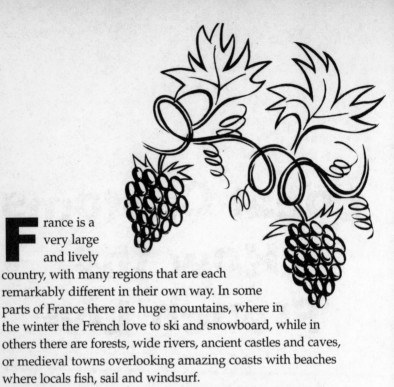

France is a very large and lively country, with many regions that are each remarkably different in their own way. In some parts of France there are huge mountains, where in the winter the French love to ski and snowboard, while in others there are forests, wide rivers, ancient castles and caves, or medieval towns overlooking amazing coasts with beaches where locals fish, sail and windsurf.

But what the French have in common throughout the country is a love of *cuisine* (a word you will hear a lot in France, it means 'food' – as well as 'kitchen' – and the different ways in which it is cooked) alongside a liking for long leisurely meals, with many courses, and a good discussion. The French love to talk!

Among other things, France is famous for its restaurants, cafés, cooking and food. So much so that a lot of words that you might have heard used in English such as 'restaurant' or 'dessert' are in fact French words that have been adopted over the centuries in other languages throughout the world. It is said that there are over 500 different cheeses made in France and some of the best wines in the world are made from grapes grown in French vineyards that stretch for miles.

Everything looks, sounds and smells different in France. One of the other things you might first notice in France is the number of cafés there are, whether you are in a big city like Paris or in a small French town or village. The café is part of the French way of life. They often open very early in the morning, and people stop in on their way to work for a coffee (the French drink a lot of strong coffee) sometimes with a *croissant* which they have just bought at the bakery (called *boulangerie* in French). It is not considered rude to eat something bought from the bakery when you're in a café,

---

Other things you might notice in France:

☞ Letter boxes and postal vans are yellow.

☞ Post offices have a blue bird logo against a yellow background. They are never found in a newsagents or a grocer's.

☞ The French don't tend to queue at bus stops, or anywhere really!

☞ You **will sometimes** see elegant ladies with fancy poodle dogs.

☞ A green cross sign lit up outside a shop is the sign for a French chemist (which is called a *pharmacie* in French).

☞ French supermarkets sell **everything**, from cups to cookers, clothes to CDs as well as food.

☞ The French say '*allô*' when they answer their telephones, but never when they say 'hello' otherwise.

What is Franglais?

Franglais is when a word or an expression is made up from a little bit of French and a big bit of English.

☞ Le blue-jeans

☞ Le weekend

☞ C'est cool

☞ Le football

Can you think of any other examples you've heard?

although you would never bring any other food into a café or restaurant.

Cafés are hectic at lunch time, when they serve a variety of dishes, and they stay open late into the night. Waiters are very skilled at carrying trays of drinks and food (sometimes one in each hand) and it is a very respected profession, which takes years of training to do properly. They are generally in waiter's uniform too. The cafés serve not only coffees and snacks, but sometimes three-course meals and they often have a bar. Children can go into any part of the café including the bar. The French like children and will make you feel welcome. So expect a little bit of head-patting and you may even find yourself being addressed with a pet name like *'puce'*

which
actually
means 'flea'
but is a nice thing to be
called!

French
people spend
a long time
over their drinks
either chatting
(sometimes
quite loudly
with lots of
hand-waving and
gestures!), reading,
or simply watching
the world go by. In the same way that the English, for example, don't all wear bowler hats, the French don't all wear berets, but in the early evening you may well see

Words that mean the same in French and English:

☞ Village

☞ Sandwich (But French sandwiches are never square!)

☞ Taxi

☞ Okay

☞ Toilettes (although spelt differently)

☞ Menu

☞ Chef

☞ Orange

☞ Train

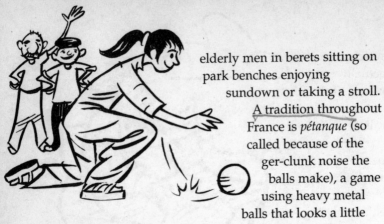

elderly men in berets sitting on park benches enjoying sundown or taking a stroll. A tradition throughout France is *pétanque* (so called because of the ger-clunk noise the balls make), a game using heavy metal balls that looks a little like bowls but is perhaps even more difficult. It is often played next to cafés in town or village squares so that people can watch the game and it is usual to see people of all ages from old men to teenagers playing alongside one another. It can be very competitive, so much so that at times the grunts and guffaws of frustration can turn the air blue when a game is lost! But because the French language sounds so lovely, you probably won't notice. Look out for the gadget that some of the very old players use to pick up the balls if they can't bend down easily. It looks like a key ring on a chain, but is in fact a very strong magnet that sticks to the ball so that it can be retrieved. You can buy them (and *pétanque* sets) in supermarkets: think of the fun you could have with that at home!

Meet and Greet

The French are quite traditional and formal in their way of greeting. It would be considered very rude not to say hello and goodbye in the right way, so even very young children learn to greet people properly. You will notice a lot of kissing in France and it is likely that if you go to a French home you will be kissed! French men tend to shake hands with one another when saying hello and goodbye. At special family occasions such as a wedding, men often kiss one another once on both cheeks if they know each other well or are related. Children tend to kiss grown-ups that they know well once on both cheeks, and women kiss both men, women and children on both cheeks. Confused? The good news is that children don't generally kiss one another until they are older, rather they say '*salut*' (sounds like 'saloo') which is a good word to have up your sleeve as it means both 'hi' and 'bye'. One word, two occasions to use it. Excellent! But you would not necessarily say that to a grown-up unless you knew them well. It would be a little like saying 'Yo' to your teacher.

A Walk Down a French Street

There are certain things you will see or come across that are done completely differently in France. The French drive on the right-hand side of the road, so to avoid being squashed you must first look left, not right! In France the pedestrian crossings do not always show a green light when it is time to cross.

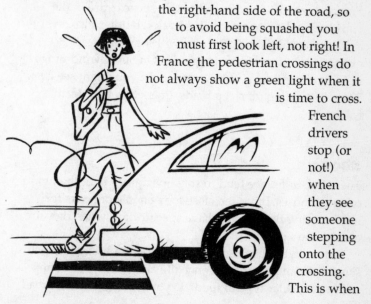

French drivers stop (or not!) when they see someone stepping onto the crossing. This is when the adult you have taken to France can prove useful and it is advisable to stick close, if not just behind them when crossing very busy roads. The French have a much faster, yet at times more leisurely way of driving and it is not unknown to see a French driver leaning out of the window to ask directions or just say hello to someone they know! Look out for the classic French car called a *deux chevaux* (so called as its engine was equivalent to the power of two horses). You might notice it because it has a roof that rolls back across the top of the car. It has often jokingly been said that these cars allowed the French to drive without their long sticks of bread (called *baguettes)* getting bent.

You will also hear the whirring sound of *mobylettes* (very small-engined scooters) a lot throughout France. If you are French you can drive one when you're 14, so lots of teenagers whiz around on them. The French are also very enthusiastic cyclists, and every year hold the Tour de France, the most famous and toughest cycle race in the world. They love to ride their bicycles, but it is also a very serious sport in France and you will see cyclists everywhere, often riding in groups. On Sunday mornings in the countryside or in the mountains, you might see 20 or 30 cyclists riding up steep roads, dressed in their team colours.

Shops

The shops in France tend to stay open much later than in other countries, but often close for a couple of hours for lunch during the day and have specific days when they are not open at all.

Although there are supermarkets, the traditional French shops are a huge part of French life and each type of shop sells a particular type of food. So you wouldn't find a bread

shop selling meat for instance. It is likely that you will notice the huge range of different smells when you visit these shops and wherever you are in France, you will see most of these shops. Whenever you go into a shop, they will always say good morning or good afternoon and it is polite to reply with *'bonjour'*, which means 'good day'. They will also usually say *'au revoir'* when you leave, which means 'goodbye'.

Charcuterie (butcher and delicatessen)
This is not unlike a butcher's, but they also sell a range of dried sausages and cooked meats, *pâté* (a delicious French meat dish) and specialities from the local region including quiche, which was invented in France. Sometimes these shops will have a big horse's head as a sign outside, the traditional sign for a butcher's shop because they really sold horse meat!

Boulangerie (bakery)
In France that there are literally hundreds of different types of loaves, rolls and pastries. After the French Revolution, the government made it a law that any village, however small, had to have a *boulangerie* and it also set the weight and price of the products sold. The French make daily trips to buy their fresh bread and the bakers are kept busy baking throughout the day.

Although you can buy it in supermarkets, sliced bread is not eaten very much in France.

Confiserie (handmade sweets and chocolates)

The *confiserie* sells handmade chocolates and sweets, often sold by weight. The smell in these shops is divine, so it's worth going to them just to breathe in deep!

Crémerie (dairy)

This is where you buy food such as butter, cream, eggs and yoghurt. A *crémerie* also sells lots of types of different cheeses, including many local specialities – made from cow's, goat's or sheep's milk depending on the local farming practice.

Fromagerie (cheese shop)

A cheese shop is different from a dairy (phew! shopping in France can be exhausting), as it tends to have a much bigger range of cheeses from all over France.

Homes and Family Life

Wherever you are in France, the buildings can vary enormously. There are medieval towns where people live in houses that are hundreds of years old, and traditional farmhouses or cottages that reflect the local region's styles and traditions. In the cities a lot of people live in apartments that are much bigger than what we know as flats and are easily large enough for families. Often these buildings are very tall with very big doors, in which there is a smaller entrance door to a shared stairway, with the apartments looking over a central courtyard. There is frequently a *concierge* (the person who looks after the building) who lives in an apartment right next to the main doorway.

Unlike Spain or Italy, grandparents do not generally live

with their families in the same house, although they often live nearby or in the same village. But there is still a strong family tradition in France. Students tend to study in their home town and live with their parents while at university.

French children are allowed to stay up quite late during the holidays, although not as late as Spanish or Italian children who often are up until beyond midnight. So you will see children playing or walking around with their parents late, after supper. Family meals are generally much bigger and last longer in France than they do in Britain, and although there is not a set day of the week for family meals there are a lot of celebrations throughout the year with different types of food. The French equivalent of an average supper of beans on toast on a school night is *jambon purée* which is ham with mashed potatoes. As school days are very long in France (children don't finish school until 4pm or 5pm), it is customary for children to have a *goûter* (which means a snack) when they get home, as supper tends to be at

☞ That the British say sorry a lot.

☞ That the British are obsessed with tea.

☞ That the British overcook food and eat a lot of roast beef, hence the nickname of 'Rosbifs' – get it?!

☞ That the British either all carry umbrellas or are dressed as farmers!

8pm with the rest of the family. A typical snack is a buttered baguette with a bar of chocolate in between. Delicious! Another thing you might notice if you go to a French home, is that considerably more families have **both** cats **and** dogs.

Weddings in France are big family occasions, although if a couple are getting married in a church, they must first marry in a Mairie (which is like a town hall) before proceeding to the church as the law in France means that everyone in France must marry in a Mairie. So they can have to marry twice in one day! Guests put a little bit of white net fabric on their car aerials in celebration, and you will often see a convoy of cars honking their horns as the wedding party and their guests drive to the reception. Other cars join in honking too and suddenly a whole town can be celebrating a wedding by sounding their car horns! At weddings or on special occasions children are normally given a little bit of wine or champagne to celebrate too.

France in its spare time

Like in any country, the French do a range of things in their spare time. Going to films, museums, listening to music, playing computer games and reading books are very popular, as is watching TV.

TV

The main TV channels in France are called TF1, France 2,
France 3, Canal + (pronounced canal ploos; it is like a cable
channel that you pay for) and La 5, which is a channel that
shows art programmes. If you happen to see French
television you will notice a lot of programmes that you have
seen at home, and that have been translated into French.
Sometimes the actors' mouths are still be moving after the
words have finished! This is because the sound has been
'dubbed', which means French actors record the words in
French over the English soundtrack. You might also see a film
or programme which is in English, but with French words, or
subtitles along the bottom translating all the speech.

France on Film

The Lumière brothers, who were French, invented the
early form of cinema just over 100 years ago. The French
have a huge film industry. A lot of French films are
subtitled or dubbed into English and other languages and
shown throughout the world. The Cannes Film Festival is
one of the most famous film festivals in the world and
has an award ceremony that is equivalent to the Oscars
(except that the awards are called
Caesars).

   The French go to the
cinema a great deal.
If you are in
France you may
well see films
that you
recognize, but
they might be
translated and called something else entirely.
Here are a few examples:

☞ *Jaws* was called *Les dents de la mer* which means 'the teeth in the sea' or 'sea teeth'.

☞ *Lord of the Rings* was called *Le Seigneur des Anneaux*. *Seigneur* is equivalent to the word Lord and *Anneaux* means Rings.

☞ *Men in Black* was called *Men in Black*! So some things really are the same.

Music

France is a nation of music lovers, and traditionally has a great love for classical music, jazz, blues and different types of music from all around the world. They even have a musical festival once a year that goes on throughout the country. Every type of music is played in France from rock to hip-hop. M. C. Solaar is a very popular rapper in France who you may come across. It is quite possible that in the supermarkets you will hear Robbie Williams singing in French on the radio! Often musicians record their songs in French, as French law only allows a certain amount of songs with English lyrics to be played each day. So if pop stars also record their music in French, it will be played more frequently. France has a big music industry of its own. One of the most recently successful bands from France is called Air.

Books

Many French people are keen book readers and some of the greatest writers have been French. There are many great French writers across the centuries from Voltaire to Proust. If you go in to a bookshop, which is called a *librairie* (no, it's not a library), you will spot books by writers you know too, but the books will have been translated into French and often have different titles.

The French also love what the British know as cartoon books, but they are considered much more important in

Brigitte Bardot

Discovered aged 19 at the 1953 Cannes Film Festival, she later became one of the most famous faces in the world. Bardot really achieved international stardom when she was in a very famous film called *And God Created Woman*. She later retired from acting and now runs the Brigitte Bardot Foundation to end cruelty to animals.

Catherine Deneuve

Born into an acting family Catherine made her first film in 1958 at the age of just 15. Considered, rightly, to be a great beauty, Catherine is one of the most famous French actresses.

Gérard Depardieu

Gérard Depardieu, with a career that began in the the 1960's, has become the most famous and successful French actor. He has not only starred in French films but has even been cast in big-budget Hollywood films as leading man, a rare achievement for a non-American. The film you are most likely to have seen him in is the 2001 film *Astérix and Obelix* in which he played Obelix. He is a massive star in France.

France and are not just for children. Adults like them too. There are many different types of books illustrated with cartoons and drawings that are popular in France and it is well worth looking through them in a French bookshop, as you will still be able to understand them. Astérix books are brilliant in any language! Another great series are the Tintin books, which were originally written in French, although actually by a Belgian, George Rémi (known as Hergé: turn

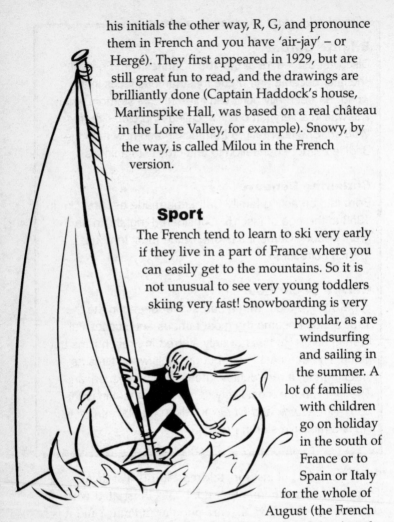

his initials the other way, R, G, and pronounce them in French and you have 'air-jay' – or Hergé). They first appeared in 1929, but are still great fun to read, and the drawings are brilliantly done (Captain Haddock's house, Marlinspike Hall, was based on a real château in the Loire Valley, for example). Snowy, by the way, is called Milou in the French version.

Sport

The French tend to learn to ski very early if they live in a part of France where you can easily get to the mountains. So it is not unusual to see very young toddlers skiing very fast! Snowboarding is very popular, as are windsurfing and sailing in the summer. A lot of families with children go on holiday in the south of France or to Spain or Italy for the whole of August (the French tend to take a month in the summer for their holidays) as the weather is so good and the south is not far by car or train.

A School Day in France

Like you, French children have to go to school whether they like it or not. And, as with all things in a different country, things are done a bit differently.

Nearly all French children go to nursery school, some starting from as young as two years old. Primary school (*école primaire*) is from six to eleven, and children have to be there 26 hours a week. The way school years are counted is the opposite from Britain, as age six to seven is their year eleven. Then, you've guessed it, the next year is year ten, and so it goes until ten to eleven, which is year seven.

The exam system is different too. If exam results across all subjects show that a child isn't doing well enough, he or she has to repeat the whole year again. This is called *redoublement* and can happen over and over again. How would you feel about that? Thought so.

In France you have to go to secondary school up to age 16, but what's different is that you take an exam at age 15 to decide whether you go on studying or not.

The years are still counted downwards from year 6 to year 1 and they end with *'la classe terminale'*.

Most children go to a state school, and usually this means a four-day week. There is generally no school on Wednesday afternoon. In Paris, though, children may have to go from Monday to Friday. The primary school day starts at 8.30 in the morning, and finishes at 4.30 in the afternoon, but from when children go to secondary school they can start as early as 8am, and not finish until 5pm, although they do have two hours for lunch. In some areas the children have to go to school on Saturday mornings, too.

But just as you were beginning to feel sorry for French children, I should tell you that they do have the longest school holidays in the world. They get 117 days (just under 4 months) in a year. Oh, and most schools don't have a school uniform!

THE HIDDEN LIFE OF Paris

There's lots to see in Paris, but there might be even more than meets the eye. For instance...

Do they come alive at night?

Notre Dame Cathedral has lots of gargoyles

Behind the church of St. Eustache, there's a giant stone head and hand

He looks deep in thought. Wonder what he's thinking of?

Then there's Père Lachaise Cemetery, where the angels are

Those stone figures on the Arc de Triomphe?

That's the past telling stories to the future

And outside the Pompidou Centre, there's the nuttiest fountain you'll ever see, with mechanical sculptures of lots of weird creatures

It's totally bonkers!

That's Paris for you – life is everywhere, including in the most unexpected places!

Fabulous Buildings and Sights

The Eiffel Tower, Paris

The Eiffel Tower should first be looked at from far away, so that you get a clear view of how tall it is and of its weird shape, like a metal giraffe. Its widely-spread legs hold up 1,063ft (324m) of metal that eventually narrows to a pointed top. You can travel nearly to the top and look out over the whole city of Paris.

But why did such a strange building ever get made in the first place? The Eiffel Tower was built by Gustave Eiffel to celebrate the centenary of the French Revolution, in 1889. It cost under 8 million francs, and 2,500,000 rivets were used in its construction. The French decided that as it was such an important thing to remember they might as well make this tower the tallest building in the world (which it was until 1930) and one of the oddest looking (which it still is). Even though it attracts millions of visitors, not everyone in Paris, or even France, is very fond of it. It was never intended to be exist forever, and shortly after it was built lots of important and famous people signed a petition, asking for it be to be torn down. Luckily for us it survived.

If you get to see it at night it looks different again, but very beautiful. It is covered in lights like an enormous metal Christmas tree. Imagine the electricity bill!

If the Eiffel Tower could talk, it could tell many very

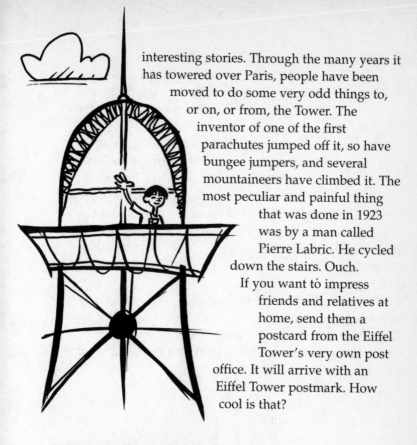

interesting stories. Through the many years it has towered over Paris, people have been moved to do some very odd things to, or on, or from, the Tower. The inventor of one of the first parachutes jumped off it, so have bungee jumpers, and several mountaineers have climbed it. The most peculiar and painful thing that was done in 1923 was by a man called Pierre Labric. He cycled down the stairs. Ouch.

If you want to impress friends and relatives at home, send them a postcard from the Eiffel Tower's very own post office. It will arrive with an Eiffel Tower postmark. How cool is that?

Mont St-Michel, Normandy

There is an island off the coast of Normandy that looks like a picture from a fairy tale. It is a huge rock really, with a beautiful medieval abbey at the top, and many smaller ancient buildings below, seemingly clinging to the rock like limpets. It is no longer an actual island, as you can walk across to it, and then continue walking up the very steep road to the abbey itself.

The unusual shape and peculiarity of the island, and the way it was so difficult to reach on foot (once, you could only cross at low tide) made it a place that religious myths grew up around, and pilgrims have journeyed to it for centuries. (A pilgrim was someone who travelled to places of particular religious importance). Often during the long climb up Mont St-Michel, pilgrims would be swept away to their death by the sea.

Supposedly the place where St Michael lived, the monastery was originally set up in his honour in the 8th century. (That's over 1,200 years ago – can you imagine?) After the French Rvolution the monks who lived there were told to leave and the monastery became a prison until 1966, when the religious people were allowed to return. Many thousands of tourists visit Mont St-Michel. A few complain about their sore feet as it is such a steep walk up, but it's well worth it!

You can watch as the tides rise up to 50ft (15m), it's quite an event as people gather each day to watch the tide come in, at first slowly and then really fast. And it really makes you understand how dangerous a journey it would once have been.

The Louvre, Paris

The Louvre, beside the Seine in the centre of Paris, was the Louvre Palace until it was turned into an art museum in 1793. It started life as a medieval fortress, and it has been rebuilt and added to over three hundred years, most famously with the addition of a big glass pyramid in 1988. It is an enormous museum that has many different art exhibitions inside. There are ancient Egyptian artefacts, beautiful dazzling collections of royal jewels, and mega-famous works of art such as the Mona Lisa, Leonardo Da Vinci's famous painting of an unknown woman smiling. It is said that at whichever angle you look at the painting of the Mona Lisa, she is looking you straight in the eye!

Le Gouffre de Padirac, southwest France

If you are lucky enough to holiday in southwest France you may well get to go on a boat-trip far below the ground. Well, 338ft (103m) below, to be exact. How can that be? Well, the area is a naturally-made enormous series of underground lakes within underground caves. You get down to the caves by going into what looks to be a hole in the ground, because that's just what it is. It's no surprise that this hole in the ground, a sheer drop down if you jumped, is called the Abyss. You travel the whole way down, by stairs or lift, and at the bottom you look up and see a beautiful circle of blue sky. Wave goodbye to the sky, as from there you go on a boat trip that takes up to one-and-a-half hours. It will feel like nothing else you have experienced before, a spooky trip to the centre of the earth.

The Statue of Liberty, Paris

Everybody knows the Statue of Liberty is in America, and so it is. The Statue of Liberty is on Liberty Island, New York.

What you may not know is that it was given to America by France, and was made in France in 1876. It was a gift intended to celebrate the centenary of America's independence from Britain back in 1776.

There are however four smaller models of the statue in Paris. (Makes you wonder if the French regretted giving the statue away, having so many reminders of it.) The biggest, though much smaller than the original, was given to the French by the Americans. With all those statues going back and forth, it's a bit like a giant game of pass-the-parcel.

The French seem to like to make their monuments as tall as possible, as the statue in New York is only a metre shorter than the Eiffel Tower, and it is still an impressive monument even when compared to the massive skyscrapers built today. One reason for the height may be that the man who was responsible for the design of the Eiffel Tower, Gustave Eiffel,

Marseilles harbour

50

was also involved in building the Statue of Liberty. He must have been a very busy man.

The Cathédrale Notre-Dame, Paris

When you go to visit this massive, amazing-looking cathedral, it is worth remembering that it is built on a spot that has had some kind of place of worship on it since Roman times. How strange to think that people have prayed, to different gods, here for thousands of years. When you get right in front of it, put your head back and look up to the top of it. The style of architecture it is built in is called Gothic, which is sometimes a term used to describe buildings in horror films, and when you see Notre-Dame you can understand why. Many consider it to be the best example of Gothic architecture, as it's intricate and detailed, and has a few surprises! When it was built, in the 12th century, it would have been the biggest thing most people had ever seen, which seems right as this was the house of their God, who was everywhere and knew everything. When it was built, a lot of the statues and carvings on the outside of the building would have been painted in bright colours.

The thing you must do is climb the 387 stairs (tiring, but definitely worth it) to the top of one of the towers to look out over Paris. Once you have taken in that view, and it really is high up, take a closer look at the weird carved stone heads known as gargoyles. That's one of the building's many surprises. They are like a stone-built version of a cross between a dragon and a prehistoric bird. How gargoyles originated remains somewhat of a mystery, but they can be found here, and similar things can be found on other Gothic churches and cathedrals all over France and elsewhere.

One theory is that the stonemasons who carved them did them partly out of mischief, giving these monsters faces that looked a bit like their bosses.

Another reason may have been as a kind of good luck charm, the gargoyles being believed to be so scary they frightened away demons who came wanting to bring ill-will to the cathedral and its worshippers.

The Pompidou Centre, Paris

When you are in Paris and have had enough of old buildings, for a complete change, take a look at the Pompidou Centre.

It is not like any building you have seen before or will see again. Its different colours might remind you of a Lego model, and it looks for all the world like it has been turned inside out. In a way that's exactly what's happened. And it really was meant to be built that way.

Opened in 1977 it was designed to provide as much space inside as possible, so the architects, Renzo Piano and Richard Rogers, put all the pipes and even the escalator on the outside of the building. The pipes holding all the necessary bits and pieces that keep the gallery lit and heated and the water supply are really big and look like you could walk through them, and in the ones that are coloured grey you can.

Montpellier at night

If you ride up the escalator you get a great view over Paris. There is even a rooftop restaurant where you can see the view from behind glass in the winter.

Inside is a modern art museum, but as many people come to look at the building itself, with buskers and portrait artists outside, as they do the exhibits. In fact the Pompidou Centre has had so many more visitors than expected that it had to be closed for repairs when the building was only a few years old.

Outside there is also a fabulously strange fountain with various odd statues spouting water, including a mermaid and a skull!

The Standing Stones at Carnac, Brittany

You probably have quite a good idea of what Stonehenge looks like. It's an odd circular arrangement of stones, some with three arranged like a kind of doorway, others all alone.

They're thousands of years old, but although they have been studied for centuries, no one is quite sure why they are there, which is part of the reason everyone likes going to Stonehenge.

If you go to an area of Brittany called Carnac however you will get to see a lot more ancient standing stones, but in a way this place is even more strange. This area has about 3,000 standing stones in all. There are three sites of these fantastic arrangements. The Alignement de Kermario, with about a thousand stones set out in ten rows, looks like a standing army. One of the many legends that have attempted to make sense of them is that they are a Roman army, turned to stone.

And it does look just like that if you look at them as the sun is going down, and the shadows start to play tricks.

They are reckoned to date from about 4500 to 2000 BC, and are therefore older than Stonehenge, and the pyramids of Egypt. These stones truly are prehistoric – like Stonehenge – and no one can really say who built them, but there is a museum called the Musée de Préhistoire that tells you masses about them.

Once you have had enough of being puzzled you can go to the nearby beach, Carnac-Plage, and the seaside resort of Carnac. We don't know who built the ancient stones, but it was nice of them to put them up so near the seaside.

The Châteaux of the Loire Valley

The river Loire is the longest river in France and lies in the Loire valley that cuts across northwestern France. It is an area of amazing natural beauty, and unusual manmade wonders as well.

This part of France is very fertile and has become famous for its wine-producing vineyards, the lush green countryside and its intriguing history. Traditionally this is where the French aristocracy built their *châteaux* (castles), which have now become huge tourist attractions, and if you only get to visit one of them you will understand why. Many are at least 700 years old, and wandering around a château, you will feel like you are walking through a fairy-tale castle. Each has real-life dramatic stories to tell, which, like fairy tales, usually involve princes and princesses, plots, and sometimes even murder.

The Château d'Azay-le-Rideau

This is one of the most beautiful of the lot as it sits on an island in the river Indre. It is built in the Renaissance and Gothic styles that look like storybook illustrations, with pointed towers, a moat, and a grand stairway wide enough for a dramatic procession.

The château dates from 1518, and belonged to a nobleman who worked for the King, Gilles Berthelot. He had to leave his home rather hastily as his cousin was involved in a financial scandal, and the King, Francois I, swiped the château for himself. It is not even certain that Berthelot had done anything wrong. You should also go to see the remains of the ancient cave-dwellers' (troglodytes') homes, that have been discovered nearby. Many of these caves have hidden entrances to protect the people who lived there from being attacked by invaders. The caves were so well hidden that they were only re-discovered about twenty years ago.

The Château d'Ussé

This pretty château is said to be the one that inspired Charles Perrault to write the story of Sleeping Beauty in the 17th century. According to legend Charles Perrault stayed in the Château while he was on his travels through France, and when he was there his imagination was fired up by the loveliness of the place. It certainly looks like that could be true, as it is built by the side of the forest of Chinon, looking over the lake, and is made of white stone.

This area has been a settlement since Viking times, but the château on the site has been built in different styles over several centuries from the 15th to the 17th. Make sure while you are there that you climb up to the round tower. There you will see a collection of scenes from the story of Sleeping Beauty represented by wax figures. After wandering around the castle and then seeing the story brought to life (well, wax) you could end up believing the story is true.

Disneyland®, Paris

This is actually about 30km outside Paris. It has a purpose-built train station, and trains connect with the Eurostar from London. It was the first Disneyland® in Europe and is just like Disneyland® in the USA, with all the characters and rides. But all the ticket-sellers speak French!

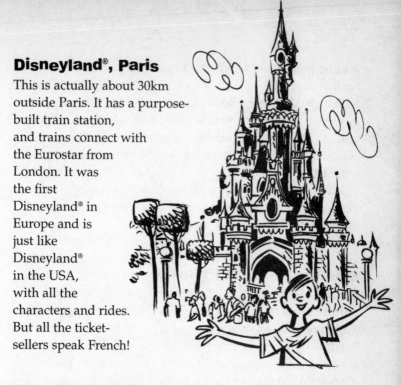

Èze, French Riviera

Èze is an ancient village, one of what the French call a *village perché*, built on top of an extremely steep hill, and it's probably unlike any place you've ever seen before, full of winding cobbled streets. You may find it hard to know where you are going, and there is a reason for that. The people of Èze built the village this way in order to confuse invaders, and if that seemed to be failing they would pour boiling oil down on them.

Cars aren't allowed into the narrow village streets, and until recently it used to be donkeys that were used to fetch and carry, but they aren't allowed in any more either – for fear of them biting the tourists, apparently (that might make you think twice about going on a seaside donkey-ride!). At night, when the cobbled streets are lit by torches and you can't hear or see any cars, you can convince yourself as you wander among the age-old buildings that you've travelled back in time.

Being so high up, about 13,000ft (4,000m), you can stand on a balcony and find yourself on eye-level with a hawk or some sea bird, with a breathtaking view of the blue sea below. It may be the nearest you get to being a bird without learning to fly.

While you are there you should see the amazing 'Jardin Exotique', a garden full of strange and colourful exotic plants on top of the highest hill in Èze.

Monaco, French Riviera

Monaco is the second smallest principality (meaning a country ruled by a prince or princess) in the world, so it's not really France at all. It is squashed against the Mediterranean Sea, it is small, measuring just 0.75 square miles (1.95 square km), and has a population of about 32,000 people. Think how strange that is: it would be like a medium-sized town in Britain deciding to have its own King or Queen.

The whole area of Monaco is urban, with no farmland at all, and it is packed with buildings, many of which are skyscrapers. There literally is no more room to build except upwards!

The Royal Family is the Grimaldi family,

who have been independent rulers here since 1419, and they have had an eventful history.

Monaco is regarded as a very glamorous place, for many reasons. Monaco has been a tax haven since 1870, which means that no one who lives there has to pay any of their money to the government – nothing at all. A nice place to be wealthy. Monaco has naturally attracted the rich and famous, and you will see beautiful yachts in the sea and beautiful designer clothes on the people.

Probably Monaco's most famous moment was in the 1950s, when Prince Rainier III married a Hollywood film star, a very beautiful and famous actress called Grace Kelly. It caused a huge amount of publicity. Was this really the romantic love story come true that could have been depicted in one of the very films that Grace Kelly had starred in when she was an actress? It seems strange to think of it now, causing so much attention, until you compare it to the British Royal Family. What would happen if Prince William really did marry Britney Spears? Yes, you would get fed up of hearing about it on the news, wouldn't you?

While you are in Monaco you will be struck by its beauty, the old white stone buildings, and palm trees, set against the bright blue sea, and if you look up, the tall modern towers that seem to want to pierce the sky. The Grimaldis' Palace

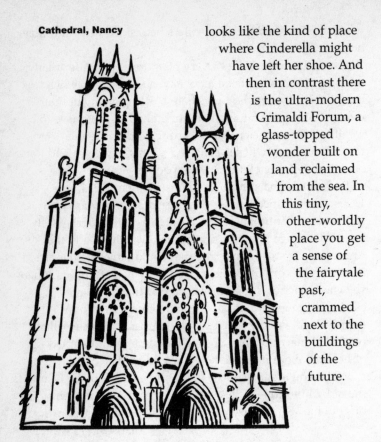
Cathedral, Nancy

looks like the kind of place where Cinderella might have left her shoe. And then in contrast there is the ultra-modern Grimaldi Forum, a glass-topped wonder built on land reclaimed from the sea. In this tiny, other-worldly place you get a sense of the fairytale past, crammed next to the buildings of the future.

Great Inventors, Famous Artists, Scientists and a Soldier

The Montgolfier Brothers

Joseph and Étienne Montgolfier were pioneers of the hot-air balloon. Nowadays it is hard to imagine how exciting it was to see a large balloon travel a few metres through the air, but to people who had no idea of flight it was both terrifying and fascinating. One of the first experimental balloons ended up being attacked by the local people when it landed. Well, if you'd never seen anything other than a bird fly, you might think that this strange round thing was a monster, mightn't you?

The hot-air balloon seems very old-fashioned to us now, but it was one of the early goes at flying. You'll often see balloon flights overhead in certain parts of France.

In 1783, the Montgolfier brothers successfully launched the first balloon to have passengers. Any guesses as to what those first passengers were? Men, women and children?

Wrong. A sheep, a duck, and a rooster were the first creatures to fly without using wings. The first flight made by actual people followed shortly after, on 21 November 1783. The balloon was built by the Montgolfier brothers, but they didn't test-fly it themselves. It makes you wonder if they weren't sure how safe it was, and it seems they had good reason as that flight nearly ended in disaster when the ropes caught fire. Oops.

The brothers' determination paid off though, and balloon flights became more and more daring and successful, until everyone started getting interested in aeroplanes instead. If you do ever get a chance to go up in a hot-air balloon, you will find it even more exciting and scary than flying by plane. And better than any ride at the fair!

The Lumière Brothers

Louis and Auguste Lumière were the first people to show a cinema film to the world, on 28 December 1895. They had invented a small 'Cinematograph', a camera that could photograph, develop and project films.

Their fascination with this subject came from their wealthy father, as they grew up watching him work at his photographic studio in Lyon. He was also interested in the current fascination with the moving image. Across the world, people got hooked on the idea, with inventors in America and Europe working on the same idea at the same time, trying to successfully develop a camera that would record moving images and then reproduce them. But the French Lumière brothers got there first. Strangely they didn't think their invention was that important, and couldn't believe that people would be that interested in films for very long. How wrong they were. They should have had a bit of a clue from the reaction people had to the first screenings. On seeing a film of a train coming out of a tunnel, their audience reacted with terror, and some ran from the room in fear. Quite a success for the first-ever action movie. The brothers also made the first comedy film, which is the famous film showing a young boy mischievously attempting to fool a gardener by stepping on the garden hose, causing the gardener to be sprayed with water.

Napoleon Bonaparte

Napoleon was one of the greatest military commanders in history. He was born in Corsica on 15 August 1769 and joined the military at an early age.

In 1796, he took command of the French army. He found an unpaid, starving, poorly equipped army on the verge of mutiny. Within days, he had organized supplies of shoes and food; and within months, his army had driven the powerful invading Austrian army out of northern Italy. He then chased it back almost to Vienna and forced the Austrians to make peace. The young general had saved France from invasion. He was only 28.

So began the legend of the astonishing man whom his soldiers called 'The Little Corporal'. There are many tales about him: that at the sound of the drums his soldiers would follow him anywhere, that his presence in his plain grey greatcoat was equal to the presence of 40,000 troops on the battlefield. It was said that he had a lucky star and that he could not be beaten. He felt that his adored wife Josephine was his talisman. In later years, when he and Josephine had parted, it was said that his luck was not the same.

Under Napoleon's command the French became a fighting force like no other. They won the Battle of Rivoli against the Austrians in 1767 by marching by moonlight at great speed, outflanking their enemy, and taking them

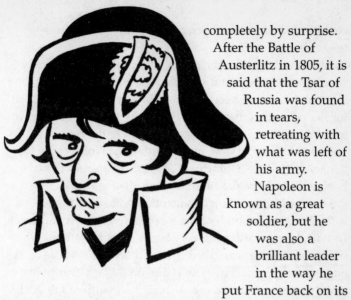

completely by surprise. After the Battle of Austerlitz in 1805, it is said that the Tsar of Russia was found in tears, retreating with what was left of his army. Napoleon is known as a great soldier, but he was also a brilliant leader in the way he put France back on its feet after the chaos of the French Revolution. In return the French people really loved him.

In 1804 he crowned himself 'Emperor of the French' and his wife Josephine 'Empress of the French'. But in 1815 he was defeated at the battle of Waterloo by the English and the Prussians. He was sent into exile on the island of St Helena where he ended his days. His body was later brought back to France where he now lies in a memorial tomb at the Hôtel des Invalides, in Paris. It is said that Queen Victoria went down into the tomb with her young son (who later became Edward VII) and told him to 'kneel to the great Napoleon'.

Marie Curie

Marie Curie, born as Marya Sklodowska in Poland in 1867, was the person who discovered radium and unlocked the mystery of how radioactive material could be useful. It is seen as one of the most important discoveries of the 20th century, and led to the invention of X-ray photos and treatments for cancer.

Marie was a brilliant child and was interested in science from an early age, but it was very unusual at that time for a woman to become a scientist. Marie had to work very hard for her education, moving to Paris and teaching in order to make ends meet while she studied for her degrees in maths and physics. In 1903 she was awarded the Nobel Prize for her achievements. Unfortunately, both Marie and her husband Pierre paid a high price for their success. Researching radiation when no one understood the health side effects meant both of them began to get tired and weak. In 1906, by now suffering very badly from radiation poisoning, Pierre was killed in a road accident. Marie carried on her research, and by now radiation therapy was being widely used to treat cancer. Although she suffered ill health for the rest of her life, she will always be remembered for her contribution to science.

Louis Daguerre

The inventor of the first form of photography, Louis Daguerre was born near Paris in 1789. He became a painter, working at painting backdrops for the theatre, which made him intrigued by the manner in which light could affect a fabric. If you leave a dyed fabric near a window, the areas in direct sunlight will change colour, or fade, over time. This is very simply how photography works. By 1839 Louis had patented his photographic process, which he called the daguerreotype. At first, taking a picture involved a long light exposure, so having your picture taken could mean sitting absolutely still for 15 minutes. Imagine that – your jaws would be stiff from grinning. Actually, on these early pictures people usually look rather serious, as if they dare not move.

As soon as the exact process became common knowledge, other inventors got working on ways to improve the image and speed of development. And they still are, with the instant digital cameras that we have today.

Sarah Bernhardt

The greatest and most famous actress of her generation, Sarah Bernhardt was born in 1844 in Paris.

She was brought up in a convent and as a teenager she decided she wanted to become a nun. Her family had other ideas and sent her instead to a theatre school. Going from the convent, being taught by nuns, to a stage school must have been a shock to the young Sarah but somehow it turned her into a great actress. She became successful very quickly, and worked in many places in Europe, including the Gaiety Theatre in London (which is still standing), and in America. She was known for her beauty and 'golden voice'.

The roles Sarah Bernhardt played were varied. She even played men in several Shakespeare plays, including

Hamlet, which caused a lot of disapproval at the time.

Like many celebrities nowadays, she became known as much for her personal life as for her acting. She liked to collect pets. She started with little dogs but soon had snakes and parrots, lion cubs and alligators – but not all of them at once, or she would have spent all her time trying to stop some of her pets from eating the others!

She liked to sleep in a coffin, which kept people talking about her. It could be said that Sarah Bernhardt was the original 'diva'. Although she carried on acting right up to the end of her life, she eventually had to act sitting down as she lost a leg in 1915. The story was that she badly damaged it jumping off stage!

Henri Toulouse-Lautrec

Henri was an artist who lived and worked in Paris, making it his business to show a side of Paris that not many people saw. He painted the cafés and music halls that were full of life and excitement but not considered very respectable at the time. It was very much the fact that his paintings were thought to be a bit rude that made them attractive to some people.

Henri was born in 1864, and suffered from ill-health for much of his childhood, finally becoming partially crippled as a teenager when he broke both legs. After this his legs didn't grow any longer and he remained very short even as an adult.

Because of his skill as a painter he moved, with his family, to Paris where he studied under a famous portrait painter, Leon Bonnat.

In those days if you wanted to become an artist, you usually had to train as an apprentice with an older, established painter. At that time Henri wouldn't have had the chance to study at an art school or university as young artists do today, which was a pity, as he and his teacher really did not get on. It is always difficult if you don't like your teachers, especially if they decide they don't like you either!

Henri's life was not without other problems, too. His paintings and sketches depicted the nightlife of Paris, in particular at the Moulin Rouge. This famous nightclub stayed open late, and offered dancers, music and drink. One of Henri's weaknesses was that he drank too much alcohol, and this, on top of his already bad health, led to his career being very short-lived. Eventually he was so ill that he had to leave the life that he loved and go back to living with his mother. He died at the very young age of 36.

The best display of his work is in the Toulouse-Lautrec Museum in Albi, the town in southern France where he was born. It contains hundreds of his pictures and when you see them you will understand why he became so famous. They are wonderfully colourful and have an amazing feeling of liveliness about them.

Claude Monet

Born in 1840 in Paris, Claude Monet was considered a difficult child. His parents hoped he would follow in his father's footsteps and become a grocer, but what he was really interested in from an early age was art. He studied in Paris and after he had done his military service he met the other artists who would become the foundation of the Impressionist movement – including Renoir and Sisley.

Instead of painting in studios, the Impressionists painted scenes taken from real life. Much of their work showed the effect of light on a subject.

Monet spent some time in England and collected ideas from artists who were creating works of art outside of the restrictive confines of the French art world. One theme of his work was to paint the same scene several times in different light, to show how things change appearance. He also became known for painting outdoors, something that was considered quite new at the time in France. In later years his eyesight was failing but he continued to paint (some say that may be why his pictures have a fuzzy quality). At first the art world didn't take him seriously, but eventually he became wealthy and respected.

Pierre Renoir

A year younger than Monet, Pierre Renoir started his artistic career decorating porcelain, but he soon began to have a passion for painting. He painted quickly, sometimes out of doors, in an attempt to catch the changing light on the subject. Like the other Impressionist painters, rather than following the old-fashioned method of a posed picture, he would paint real-life situations, such as people going about their everyday lives, often at leisure. A very famous Renoir for instance depicts a girl watching a show at the theatre. What is striking about his works is the sense of light and movement they capture.

Louis Braille

Louis Braille was born in 1809, but at the age of three he had an accident that left him blind. In 1819 he went to the Paris Blind School, but although he could learn a certain amount, he wanted to be able to find things out for himself rather than depend on other people to read to him for the rest of his life.

You might not have heard of Louis Braille, but you will have heard of his invention, Braille. Braille is the method of writing words down, in a system of raised dots, which allows blind people to be able to read and write using their fingers and sense of touch. It is such a brilliant idea that it is hard to believe that it wasn't invented until the 19th century (although at that time a lot of people who could see were unable to read or write!). There was already a simple system of reading embossed letters, that is normal letters were written and raised from the page so that they could be felt (a bit like embroidered letters). But Louis's system was much more clever. It was quicker to read because he invented a new type of coded alphabet, using six dots in different combinations, and it could be taught to people so they could easily write for themselves.

Louis had been determined to make reading possible, both for himself, and for other people who couldn't see, and as a result he had invented Braille.

Louis Pasteur

You probably drink milk every day, and everyone tells you that it's good for you (any type of milk – cow's, goat's or sheep's), but there was a time when milk could not always be relied upon to be so healthy. Milk, after all, comes from an animal and isn't always terribly clean. The man who made it possible to drink milk that was clean and healthy was a brilliant scientist, Louis Pasteur. He was born in 1822, in a place called Dôle, in eastern France. He studied science and was making amazing discoveries from an early age. By the time he was 26 he had changed the basis of scientific thinking in chemistry.

71

He did in fact do a lot to increase modern knowledge, not just make milk drinkable. His discoveries have saved many lives. Louis worked out that tiny living things called microbes could multiply and cause disease and decay. He also discovered that, by heating food (such as milk) that these microbes were in, they could be killed off without harming the food.

That is why most milk is what we call 'pasteurized', after Louis Pasteur. Before you drink milk it is heated enough in the dairy to get rid of any microbes that might harm you.

He saved further lives by applying this knowledge to hospitals. Up till then, people working in hospitals weren't always that careful to wash their hands or clean the instruments after they had been used for operations. Yuck! So that meant a lot of people became ill or even died, as infections could easily be transferred from one person to another. Louis's discoveries led to people being able to understand how germs could be carried, and made hospitals a much safer place.

François Rabelais

The first great French writer of the 16th century, François Rabelais was a satirist. A satirist is someone who uses his comic, and often quite cruel, stories (satires) to criticize the society in which he, or she, lives. François was born in 1493, in the Loire area, and started out as a monk. He became unhappy with life in a monastery and asked the Pope for permission to leave, then went on to study medicine instead. It seems that medicine was not the right career for François either, as he started to write and publish the satires that were to make him famous, though not always the best kind of 'famous'.

The important people of the day did not like to be satirized. The main thing that annoyed people was his very modern view that people had a right to individual freedom. At a time when ordinary people had few rights at all, his ideas were seen as dangerous and revolutionary. How strange to think of a man who started life as a monk being seen, by the end of it, as something of a dangerous menace. At times he only narrowly escaped being put to death for his ideas. Aren't you glad you live now? He influenced French writing and thinking, and he gives the English language the word Rabelaisian, used to describe something that's rude and boisterous.

Coco Chanel

Many people know the name Chanel first as a perfume, the extremely expensive and always popular Chanel No 5. Nowadays it seems that every famous singer or actress is selling a perfume with their name on it (think of J. Lo and Elizabeth Taylor), but the first person to ever to launch a 'celebrity perfume' was the world-famous clothes designer, Coco Chanel.

She was born as Gabrielle Bonheur Chanel in Saumur in 1883 (though she always claimed to be ten years younger). Gabrielle adopted the nickname Coco when she had a brief career as a cabaret singer, but soon she had branched out into designing clothes.

Her first venture was a hat shop opened in 1909, but she soon became known for her ability to design comfortable and practical clothes for women. It is hard to understand now, but in the early part of the 20th century the sight of a woman in a pair of trousers was very shocking. Up until then, clothes for women had been uncomfortable and difficult to move around in. Almost every woman wore a corset under her clothes. This was a stiff undergarment that was fastened tight to make a woman's body the 'right' shape, but it also made eating and breathing difficult too – imagine not being able to finish your dinner, or run up the stairs!). Now, against all tradition, this woman designer was making soft comfortable clothes for women, and wearing exactly what she liked herself. It was something people began to talk about.

As a result, Coco Chanel became very famous, and influenced women's fashions for decades. In 1917 she had her hair cut into a 'bob', which was immediately very fashionable – again this was a style that was very new and very different. Until the bob, where hair is cut to one length and worn loose around the face, women wore their hair piled up on top of their heads in public and kept it in place with pins. (Ouch!)

So, you can see how Coco Chanel became popular, especially with women. Suddenly fashions for hair and clothes were attractive and practical, and women were able to spend less time getting dressed, and more time doing things.

A Spoonful of French Music

Edith Piaf

Edith Piaf was known as 'the little sparrow' as she was small and thin, but had the most amazing singing voice. She became an international star against all the odds, being born into a poor family living in a very poor area of Paris. Born as Edith Giavanna Gassion in 1915, she was abandoned by her mother when very young and left by her father to be brought up by relatives. Her father was an acrobat, and she became used to the touring life from an early age. By the time she was a teenager she was earning her living singing on the streets.

From this difficult beginning Edith became an ambitious singer and by 1937, aged only 22, she was singing at the top music hall in Paris, the ABC. Her ability to sing to huge numbers without a microphone, using the powerful voice she had developed singing in the street, amazed the public and from then on her success was assured. There was, however, more to Edith than her ability to entertain. During the Second World War she managed to use her celebrity status to get access to prisoners detained by the Nazis, as she toured the prisons as an entertainer, and was able to help many to escape.

After the war she became a star in America, and in 1948 in Britain, as her recording of 'La Vie en Rose' became a big hit, and is the song she is most remembered by today, along with 'Je ne regrette rien' ('I regret nothing').

Serge Gainsbourg

The man credited with bringing reggae to France, Serge
Gainsbourg, like Edith Piaf, had a tricky start in life. His real
name was Lucien Ginsburg and he was born in 1928. Being
the child of Russian-Jewish immigrants was not easy in
France during the Second World War, when the Nazis put
great numbers of Jews to death. But his family managed to
survive the Nazis.

He began as a songwriter for other musicians, but what
he really wanted to do was to perform. So in the 1950s he
changed his name to Serge Gainsbourg (to sound more
French; times were still difficult for people who had come

from other parts of Europe then) and by 1958 had released
his first record. His fame and popularity grew slowly, but he
eventually built up a massive following as his songs –
tuneful, sad, but a little funny – were perfect for France in
the years following the Second World War. By the time the
1960s were in full swing, he had become a mainstream star,
helped by his unfailing ability to shock the public! In the 60s
Gainsbourg began to become famous outside of France, and
is still a household name across much of the rest of Europe
and Britain, as he continued to produce music that was
relevant to its time throughout the 1970s and 80s. Although
Gainsbourg died some time ago, he is still considered a huge
hero in France.

Josephine Baker

An amazing woman of achievement by any standards,
Josephine Baker was a black dancer and singer who was
born in St.Louis, Missouri, America in 1906. She was well
known in America, but she became a massive star in France.
She made France her home and the French people took her
to their hearts. She first appeared in 1925 at the famous Paris
cabaret Les Folies Bergère, dressed in little more than a skirt
made from bananas! And it is still possible to see a film of
her first performance. By the 1930s she was rich and famous
enough to move her family to be with her in France.

During the Second World War she worked for the French
Resistance (the French organization who were trying to free
themselves of German occupation) and as a result she was
awarded the Légion d'Honneur (rarely given to anyone who
is not French) in recognition of her bravery.

In her busy life she managed to marry five times, to adopt
12 children, and to work with other people fighting for
freedom and rights for black people (among them Martin

Luther King) to help to bring an end to segregation in America. She died in her sleep aged 68, and is buried in Monaco.

Air

Air is a French electro-pop music duo (Nicholas Godin and J. B. Dunkel) with a worldwide following. Considered to be innovators in their field with many imitators of their distinctive sound, they really came to British attention when their first album immediately stormed the charts upon its release in 1998.

Their first album *Moon Safari* was highly critically acclaimed both in France and in Britain and America. They released their third album, *Talkie Walkie* in 2004. The dreamy music has been perfect for use in Hollywood film soundtracks, and has helped to bring them an American following. This makes Air currently the most successful French band in the world.

Food
and Drink

Meal times are important occasions in France. Everyone stops for at least an hour at lunch (*déjeuner*) and supper (*dîner*), even if it is a simple meal during the week, and dinner is usually served sitting at a table. It is usual to say *'bon appétit'*, which means 'enjoy your meal'.

Breakfast Children tend to drink milk or chocolate milk for breakfast. Another popular 'drink' is a yoghurt drink that is halfway between a milk shake and yoghurt. The French often drink from bowls at breakfast, rather than from cups or glasses. French breakfast is never a cooked meal like bacon and eggs, and the French don't really eat 'toast' in the way the British or Americans do. Traditionally the French will eat *croissants, pains au chocolat* (a bit like croissants but with

chocolate in them) or *baguette* (the very long bread we sometimes call a 'French stick') and jam at breakfast. Sometimes you also get cheese or cold meat.

Boulangeries (bakeries) open very early in France and many people go there to buy bread freshly made that morning. Cereals and yoghurt are also very popular. Adults will tend to have coffee – if you want a large, white coffee, ask for *café crème* (with cream) or *café au lait* (milky coffee), because if you just ask for a *café* you'll get a much smaller cup of strong, black coffee.

Croissants *and* baguettes

There are many myths to do with *croissants* and *baguettes*. It is said that bread baked in the distinctive long shape of the *baguette* first came about so that Napoleon's army could carry their bread in their trousers! *Croissant* means 'crescent': the shape is said to come from the crescent moon that's pictured on the Turkish flag. No one knows where or when the first *croissant* was actually baked, but the word was first used in a dictionary in 1863 and the first recipe was published in 1891, although then it was more like a heavy cake than the flaky, scrumptious *croissant* we now know!

The great French Toast Mystery:

In Britain, 'French toast' means a type of toasted bread, which is crunchy and resembles a slice of bread.

In America, 'French toast' means bread soaked in egg and cooked (which is 'eggy bread' in Britain, but that's a different story!).

In France, bread is rarely toasted and eaten as a snack. What is often referred to as 'French toast' in Britain is called a *biscotte* in France.

So be careful what you ask for!

Lunch Often the French will lunch in cafés or local restaurants (although there are canteens at school, older children often go to cafés too). A typical lunch might be a *'plat de jour'*, which means 'dish of the day' and will always be made from fresh, local produce. Another delicious lunch-time snack that can be eaten more quickly is a *croque monsieur*. This is not unlike cheese on toast, but with ham as well as cheese between the two slices of toasted bread. A *croque madame* is the same thing, but with an egg on top! *Steak haché frites* means minced steak and chips and is often served at lunch.

Dinner This is usually served a little later than you might be used to at home, around 8–8.30pm, and children normally eat with their parents. Dinner is a main dish with salad (French children eat a lot more salad that you probably do), potato or pasta (the French eat quite a lot of pasta too) and vegetables.

Eating out

The French are a nation of great chefs, and love their food. If you are lucky enough to have eaten in a swanky restaurant,

you might have seen some
star stickers
in the
window.
This means
that the
restaurant
has been
awarded a
Michelin
star, which is
the sign of an
extremely
good

restaurant. It is the expert French chefs who decide which restaurants around the world receive this great honour and can therefore display one, two or three stars!

When not eating at home, French families often eat out in restaurants, both at lunch time and in the evening because the food is so good and such great value. You'll see many more restaurants in France than at home, even in small towns. Families tend to eat out all together and French children are generally more adventurous in their choice of food, usually eating the same food as their parents. Tomato

---

Marmite:

A *marmite* is the name of the traditional pot used for cooking meats and stews. Before cookers were invented it was traditional to use a *pot au feu*, which meant a pot hanging over the fire. It is still a technique used today, cooking meat slowly in a sauce for several hours. Once the meat is cooked, the juices are often used to make soup.

French food you might want to try:

☞ *Cassoulet* – This is a fantastic stew with pork, sausage and 'haricot' beans called (that look a little like baked beans, but taste completely different). It is a dish from the south of France.

☞ *Soupe de poisson* – This is fish soup, which might sound a bit poisonous but is very tasty indeed. It is served with a special sauce and with *croûtons* (which are little bits of toasted bread). Normandy, Brittany and the south of France are particularly well known for their fish soup.

☞ *Crêpe* – This word might make you giggle. *Crêpes* are like pancakes. In France they are served with both savoury fillings like cheese (so are good for vegetarians) as well as sweet things like syrup. Brittany is particularly known for its *crêpes*, but they are served throughout France and there are even special restaurants called *crêperies*!

☞ *Gratin dauphinois* – Mighty tasty potatoes baked in a creamy sauce.

---

ketchup is frowned upon in good restaurants, and even now French restaurants often won't serve it! On a sign outside restaurants there are usually several menus with a price marked on each. So you can choose what you are going to eat right from the beginning of the meal and know exactly how much it will cost. The menu you pick even includes your pudding! Depending on where you are in France, the restaurant will have different types of food reflecting the local area and its traditional dishes.

A typical French menu

In a restaurant there are often many courses. Here is a taster:

- ☞ *Hors-d'oeuvre*: small appetizers.
- ☞ *Entrée*: fish or eggs, or a 'light' meat.
- ☞ **Main course:** usually meat, fish or pasta salad.
- ☞ **Cheese course:** Local cheeses, sometimes followed by a green salad.
- ☞ **Dessert:** something sweet like a gooey cake (*gâteau*) or a pastry (*pâtisserie*) from the region.

Unusual food

Surely no one really eats frogs and snails? Well, the French do (but not all the time!) and they are both considered to be delicacies. If you get the chance, try eating snails (*escargots*) or frogs (*grenouilles*). They taste much better than you'd expect and are often served in the most delicious sauces.

A lot of restaurants, especially near the coast, specialize in seafood, which in French is called *fruits de la mer* (which means 'fruit of the sea'). You will see people sitting at table sucking all kinds of seafood from the shell and using their fingers to pick the seafood off the plate. Eating certain foods with your fingers is not considered bad manners in France. If you eat seafood such as prawns or lobster you will be given a bowl of water with a slice of lemon in it. This is not to be drunk! It is so that you can dip your fingers into it and clean them before the next course.

Drinks

Citron pressé and *orange pressé* (which means squeezed lemon and squeezed orange) are really thirst-quenching drinks you can get in most cafés. These drinks are made from the juice of a whole lemon or orange and served with a bottle of water and sugar. So you pour water in to dilute the juice and add a little sugar.

A lot of bottled water is drunk in France. If it is fizzy, it is *l'eau gazeuse* (water with gas). If it is still, it is called *l'eau plate* or *l'eau non gazeuse* (without gas). So the gas thing is quite a big issue!

Hot chocolate, Iced T in a can (Iced T with different flavours like lemon or peach) and nearly all the other drinks that you might have at home are all drunk by the French. One thing to look out for is Cacolac, which doesn't sound that good, but is a really nice iced-cold chocolate milk drink served in a dark brown bottle.

═ *Things you might notice in a French restaurant:* ═

☞ Bread is always served with meals, but rarely butter, as it is not customary in France to put butter on bread at main meals.

☞ Cheese is served **before** not after pudding, so that a sweet taste is left in your mouth at the end of the meal.

☞ If a dish has '*maison*' next to it, it means that it is a speciality of the restaurant and will be particularly good.

☞ Ice cream or sorbet is often served with a glass of water to help bring out the flavour.

Festivals and National Celebrations

There are 13 national holidays in France. France is historically a Catholic country so a lot of these are special religious days, such as All Saints' Day on November 1st. A lot of people also celebrate 'name days'. 27 July is Sainte Natalie, so on that day it's the celebration of all girls and women named Natalie. The French like celebrations and parties! Other celebrations are days recalling big events from French history, such as Bastille Day every July, or bank holidays where there are big celebrations in the streets.

On these holidays most shops and places such as museums shut, but this is made up for by the celebrations that take place. Even small towns throw street parties or parades and the local people may dress up. They certainly aren't boring days.

As well as national holidays that take place across the whole of France there are also local fairs and festivals, that make the most of what that area is known for, such as a certain wine or cheese. There are in fact festivals celebrating almost everything: music, art, food, wine, animals... In Dijon, they even combine music with food, and have the International Folk and Wine Festival. You could be forgiven for thinking that the French will make any excuse to have a party, but that seems to be quite a nice way to live, doesn't it?

Bastille Day: 14 July

Bastille Day celebrates the beginning of the revolution in 1789 that led to the end of the monarchy in France. It is a very important day in the French calendar, and they really do stage huge events. The celebrations start the night before, all over the country, but the best place to be is Paris as then you may get to see the military parade down the great wide Champs Élysées. Not that you will probably get much of a view as it will seem that everybody else in Paris is there too.

The city seems to go a bit crazy, as from the night before people will have been out on the streets holding parties, and there are dances held in fire stations. A strange place for a party you may think, and not a night you would want to have a proper fire emergency!

On the night of Bastille Day bonfires are lit, and fireworks are let off all over the country, in a similar way to Guy Fawkes Night in Britain, and this recreates the noise of gunfire, and explosions of the cannons, that occurred on the actual day in 1789. The difference being that in Britain fireworks on 5 November re-create what might have been, rather than what happened, as Guy Fawkes was caught before he could cause any damage. But in Paris, the explosions really did go off.

The fireworks in Paris are a huge, amazing noisy display, held in the Trocadéro in the middle of the city, but you will be able to see and hear them from just about everywhere even if you can't get very near because of the crowds.

These are the traditional celebrations, but each year something different and new may be added. One year the President decided that France should stage one huge picnic. It stretched the length of the country (about 1,000km), and was called 'the incredible picnic'. The idea was for people to share their food and drink with each other in the true spirit of the revolution, as a tribute to the idea of fraternity (brotherhood) and to a revolution that had created a France where no one would ever starve again.

Christmas and New Year

Christmas and New Year are celebrated on the same day, but for children in France present time starts earlier in December. Father Christmas, or *le père Noël*, brings them small presents on 6 December (the feast day of St Nicholas, who is the original Santa Claus, or Father Christmas), and then they receive their bigger, proper presents at Christmas. It is almost like they have a small practice Christmas before the big day.

On Christmas Eve you may be used to hanging up your stocking, or pillowcase, for Father Christmas, but French

children put out their shoes for him to fill with gifts (they can't be big enough, surely?). They also believe that not only does Father Christmas bring presents, but sometimes *le petit Jésus* (Baby Jesus) brings them too. Christmas in France is especially important for children. In fact, many parents often wait until New Year's Eve (*la Saint-Sylvestre*) to open their presents, as New Year's Eve is more special for adults. Do you think you could wait that long without taking a peek at your prezzies?

Even Christmas dinner is just as rich and filling, but a little different. There's meat as a main course, but not turkey, while the pudding is a yule log (which is more of an iced cake than a pudding). And it's all eaten at midnight on Christmas Eve, not on Christmas Day. So that would make a difference from being too excited to get to sleep on Christmas Eve, and being told to go to bed. After staying up that late, and eating all of that, you'd be happy to lie down. That all sounds like a fantastic Christmas, doesn't it?

La Fête des Rois – 6 January

La Fête des Rois (the festival of Kings) marks Epiphany, which is celebrated on 6 January by most families in France, whether they are religious or not. A traditional *galette* is eaten and there is often a family meal and celebration.

Cards

Whereas birthday cards or Christmas cards are usual in other countries, the French don't send a card to friends and relatives at Christmas, but it is traditional to send cards in the New Year, these are called 'cartes de vœux'.

Birthdays

In France there is a great tradition of the '*cadeau*', which means a 'present'. If you buy something in a shop, they may well ask you whether it is a gift and if it is they will wrap it so that it looks amazing! You would always take a birthday present to a friend's birthday party in France, but birthday cards are not generally given or sent.

Fête de la Musique

This is a truly huge nationwide event and one that, if you are there, you will be very glad to have been in France for. This festival takes place on the longest day of the year, 21 June, and unlike most of the fêtes and feast days in France it is a fairly new tradition. It began in 1982, when the director of music and dance in France, Maurice Fleuret, had a survey done and discovered that five million French people, including one in two children, played a musical instrument. That's a lot of music lessons.

As a result he started the Fête de la Musique that seeks to

encourage musicians to jam, whether professional or amateur. All over France you will hear and see musicians play every type of music you can think of – classical, dance, pop and rock. There will be a lot of traditional folk music, particularly in the smaller towns, but one of the biggest events is the rock concert held at *La Place de la République* in Paris, that attracts huge crowds, and bands from all over the world. In the year 2000, for instance, Oasis played to 4,000 people for free at this event. Who knows what singers or bands you might get to see if you are there for the festival this year?

Markets

In France markets (*marchés*) are an important part of life. Most towns and villages will have regular markets, often several different types of market every week, which are bustling and colourful occasions where lots of different things are sold. Vegetables, fish, cheeses (lots of different cheeses, some of which you will never have seen before), breads of all different shapes and sizes, and sometimes flowers. Many of these markets will also have a wide range of local meat and fish from lobsters, crabs and snails to duck and rabbits. Or soaps, honey, herbs and tarts all made locally. Much fresh food is bought at market very early in the mornings, and if you get up early enough, you will see one of the noisiest and most interesting ways of shopping. Markets are a great way of learning about the French way of life and are fantastic places just for watching and listening to people.

Sometimes the people buying will haggle with the stallholder. It doesn't happen everywhere, but it's fascinating to watch if it does. Depending on where you are, it is a normal way of agreeing a price. The stallholder will say a price, the person buying will say something back, then as this continues the customer may shake their head and start to walk away from the stall. Usually at this point the stallholder will shout out a lower price in an attempt to bring the customer back to buy, which generally works. If you fancy trying this out yourself, it's worth remembering you should only have a go at haggling in markets.

It is usual in France, for market stallholders to let you try some of the foods they are selling and there will often be little sticks for you to taste different foods. It's a great way to become familiar with French food.

Markets in Paris

Le Marché aux Fleurs is a regular flower market, from Monday to Saturday in an area called Louis-Lépine. It is worth going for the sights and smells of the beautiful flowers and plants on sale. If you go to the same place on a Sunday, you won't see any flowers, but lots of exotic birds in cages, and other animals such as mice, hedgehogs, skunks and even the familiar guinea pig. On Sundays the market is called the 'Marché aux Oiseaux'.

Le Marché aux Puces means literally 'flea market', so called because so many of the antique and second-hand goods were considered to be full of fleas. These markets really are worth going to, as they are a fascinating mix of old clothes, pictures, furniture and toys. Every city or town is likely to

have a flea market but the biggest and the most famous is the Marché aux Puces de la Porte de St Ouen, in Paris. It is thought to be the biggest market of this type in the world. It has thousands of stalls and shops, selling just about everything you can think of. You need a few hours to wander round it, and although you may not buy much, there's a lot to look at. Haggling is again something that you will see people doing, and something worth trying yourself because at this type of market the idea really is to try to find a bargain. The main street of the market is rue des Rosiers, and it is a bit of a walk from Clignancourt Métro station.

Foire à tout

More a kind of boot sale (*foire à tout*). At these markets you will see people selling all of their unwanted bits and bobs on a stall. It can often look as if someone has quite simply emptied the house of everything that no longer works! It may not look at first glance as if there may be anything you want, but it is worth having a rummage.

Also, if you want to find out more about the country you are staying in, it's a great way of finding a souvenir that will be far more original than the usual plastic model of the Eiffel Tower that everyone else seems to bring back from France.

A Little Bit of Sport

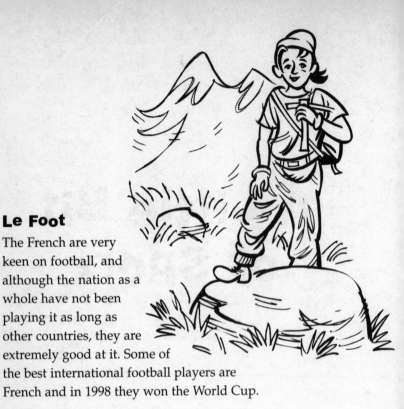

Le Foot

The French are very
keen on football, and
although the nation as a
whole have not been
playing it as long as
other countries, they are
extremely good at it. Some of
the best international football players are
French and in 1998 they won the World Cup.

A few football clubs

Olympique de Marseille play in Ligue 1, the French
equivalent of the Premiership. They are a very successful
team in France, and over the years have won 10 French
championships, as well as the European Champions League
in 1993.

Paris Saint Germain play at the Parc des Princes (the
Park of Princes) in Paris. They were founded in 1970, but
have been in Ligue 1 since 1974. As well as winning the
Coupe de France (The French Cup) five times, they also won
the European Cup Winners' Cup in 1996!

Just a few of the best French footballers

Arsène Wenger

Arsenal's manager since 1996, he made his name managing Monaco. Several French players have been signed by Arsenal on his recommendation, including Patrick Vieira and Rémi Garde.

Glen Hoddle was quoted as saying: 'I would not be where I am today if it were not for Arsène Wenger'. You can't really pay someone more of a compliment than that.

Thierry Henri

Arsenal's striker, who many consider to be the best in the world. Born in Paris, he was signed by Arsenal in 1999, having previously proved himself by being the top scorer for his country in the 1998 World Cup. He has also appeared in car adverts, but we hope he will be remembered more for his football talents.

Patrick Vieira

He joined Arsenal in 1996, was a World Cup winner with France in 1998, and was the youngest-ever French team captain when he played for Cannes, aged 19. So I suppose he's quite good then.

Eric Cantona

Perhaps still one of the most famous French footballers to play in Britain. Cantona played for both Manchester United and Leeds United and was voted Footballer of the Year in 1996. He liked to write poetry and was known for his 'philosophical' ways (he liked to think deep thoughts!) and was often quoted in newspapers saying things about birds and fishing boats that no one understood! He was very popular with the English fans. When he came on to the

pitch, football fans would shout 'Ooh-aah Cantona!' While with Manchester United he scored 80 goals. Eric Cantona retired in 1997, but remains a legend and is quite unlike any other football player. More recently he has also acted in feature films.

Rugby

It is said that rugby is like a religion in certain parts of France. The French national team is one of the best in the world. Most of the rugby played is rugby union (15-a-side) but there is some rugby league played (13-a-side). Unlike in Britain, rugby in France doesn't tend to get played in schools and universities, though it is played in clubs across the country and in particular it is the sport of the southwest region where just about every town has a team (the southwest is often called *L'Ovalie*, which means the land of the oval ball!). There is even a church dedicated to the sport of rugby called Notre Dame du Rugby at Larrivière, in the valley of the Adour river!

Skiing and other winter sports

France is about the best place to go skiing. Skiing is not just for foreigners either, as many French people love to ski in their own country.

Because of its perfect selection of mountain ranges, mostly in the Pyrenees and the Alps, there are many purpose-built resorts, and some much older traditional ski villages, which are very pretty. The slopes are graded in terms of difficulty, so that you will know where it is safe to learn, and where it is only safe for a professional-level skier. The very first time you go up the slopes in a ski lift you might find it pretty scary, and you may wish to stick to something safer, such as throwing snow-balls.

Even if you don't do much actual skiing, there will be all sorts of other snow sports going on, such as snowboarding, tobogganing and bobsleighing.

There is also quite a lot of opportunity to go ice-skating, many towns and resorts have outdoor ice-rinks in the winter. And you don't even need to be in what is considered a snow sports area: even Paris has several ice rinks.

Summer in the Mountains

In the summer, when the snow has melted, a lot of people go mountaineering or walking in the Alps and in the Pyrenees, along with cycling of course!

Pétanque

Pétanque is a bit like bowls but the *boules* (balls) are shiny stainless steel and the ground it is played on more like a sand-pit than a lawn. The ball is thrown slightly differently too, as it's given more of an underarm spin rather than the gentle roll you tend to see on an English green. The game varies a little from region to region. Generally the aim will be to hit the wooden jack (*cochonnet*) that is thrown into the middle of the playing area at the beginning of each game.

Some versions allow the player to take a small run-up before throwing the *boule*, others require them to keep their feet together (and hopefully their balance) as they throw. The game is played by two teams of two or three players.

Boules:

Trivia fact about *boules*: the word *cochonnet*, the name of the wooden jack or marker all the players are trying to hit, actually means 'piglet'. I suppose using a real one would make it much more difficult.

Cycling and the Tour de France

Cycling is more popular in France than anywhere else in the world. You will see many cyclists, and there are cycle lanes in most areas. In country areas there are wonderful quiet places to ride, though you need to take special care about traffic being on the other side of the road. The Tour de France, which takes place in July, is world famous, and is one of the most gruelling sporting events that you can imagine. The race consists of three weeks of racing nearly every day, usually covering about 4,000km altogether and climbing the massive mountain ranges of the Alps and the Pyrenees. The end of the race is always on the Champs-Elysées in Paris, but the route and

length of the race always varies a little from year to year. It has even included bits of other countries!

Millions of people around the world watch the Tour de France on television. You may have seen it yourself, and not realized how many other people are following it at exactly the same time, and not just at home. In bars, cafés, and shops all over France, during the race, televisions will be showing it. Millions of people come out to see it pass, lining the sides of the roads to catch the cyclists whizzing past (you might even be able to cheer them on if you are in France in July). As a spectator sport it can be more exciting to watch than you might expect.

Bungee-jumping

Not really a sport, is it? But it is something that has become very popular in France. If you are wise you will take to watching rather than doing, at least until you are considerably older. Bungee-jumping weekends have become a kind of extreme-sports tourism, with the bungee-jump platforms making the most of the amazing French terrain.

Odds
and Ends

The Paris sewers

In Paris there is a museum devoted to the sewers that run beneath it. Yes, you did read that right, a museum that tells you everything you might want to know about the history of removing human waste from the toilets of Paris. Not very inviting is it?

The Musée des Égouts, as it is called, has been a big attraction in Paris for the last hundred years, and until the 1970s it was possible to ride around the sewers in a boat. No, this is not a joke – the entrance to the museum is built into the underground sewers themselves. Although you can no longer take the boat-trip (yes, I know you're disappointed about that), you do get to stand on a kind of metal bridge and watch (and smell) the sewage rushing through the tunnels under your feet.

The trip round the museum is very informative and tells you everything you need to know about how the sewers work. There are people there to answer your questions.

Dom Perignon

When you are in France, you will see a lot of people drinking wine, and buying wine, and you may even be allowed to try a little. The French love wine, and there are many types, but the most expensive on the menu is usually champagne. It's the stuff you see racing drivers drench one another in when they've won their race. What a waste.

What you may not have heard is that the man credited with inventing the method for fermenting champagne (it's a very complicated process to make normal wine turn fizzy) was a monk.

His name was Dom Perignon, and that is now the name of a type of champagne.

Selling the Eiffel Tower

If I told you the Eiffel Tower, that you may have gone to the top of and taken photos of, had twice been sold for scrap, you would probably think I was fibbing. Well, I'm not. (Being sold for scrap is what happens to old cars – they are sold to someone who will take them apart to use the parts or metal – surely not to the Eiffel Tower?)

There was a scoundrel who made a lot of money by selling the Tower to gullible people. His name was Victor Lustig, and he was from Prague. In 1925 he was in Paris and decided to set up a scam. He was given the idea by an article in a newspaper that said that it cost more to maintain the Eiffel Tower than it was really worth (it had not always been a popular monument after all) and that it needed lots of expensive repairs doing to it.

So, feeling that the mood of the people would be in his favour, Victor

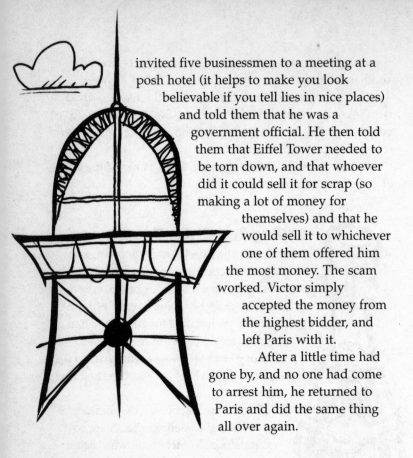

invited five businessmen to a meeting at a posh hotel (it helps to make you look believable if you tell lies in nice places) and told them that he was a government official. He then told them that Eiffel Tower needed to be torn down, and that whoever did it could sell it for scrap (so making a lot of money for themselves) and that he would sell it to whichever one of them offered him the most money. The scam worked. Victor simply accepted the money from the highest bidder, and left Paris with it.

After a little time had gone by, and no one had come to arrest him, he returned to Paris and did the same thing all over again.

The Count of Monte Cristo

The Count of Monte Cristo is a book written by Alexandre Dumas, which is such a popular story it has been made into many films. You may have even seen a cartoon version. What you may not know is that the story was based on real-life events.

This exciting tale of adventure, wrongful imprisonment and revenge has been changed a bit from the true story, but the basic facts are the same. An innocent man called Pierre Picaud had the misfortune to have some friends who didn't understand that practical jokes can go too far.

There is a wedding tradition you will have heard of called a 'stag night', when the husband-to-be goes out before his wedding day, to celebrate with his friends. Part of the tradition is that practical jokes will often be played on him. In the case of Pierre Picaud this really was the case.

Before Pierre got married, his so-called friends decided that it would be funny (for them, not Pierre) to write a letter to the authorities claiming that Pierre was a spy. Unfortunately the letter was believed and he was thrown into jail for seven years. Imagine seven years in jail for nothing – you'd be quite cross when you were let out, wouldn't you? Well, that was exactly how Pierre felt. All he could think about when he was in jail was how he could get revenge on the friends who had wronged him, and he went on thinking that way when he was free. He became quite a famous criminal as he went about doing all the things he had dreamt of.

There is some good to come out of this grim tale, however (though a bit late for Pierre).

Alexandre Dumas' book was so famous that it changed people's views, with the result that people couldn't get thrown into prison so easily. The French authorities became more aware of the need for changes in the legal and prison systems.

Michelin Man

In France you will often see the cartoon-like character of a big man in a tyre suit! This is the 'Michelin man', a man supposedly made from a stack of tyres. He is actually one of the oldest advertising logos in the world, dating from 1898, when one of the Michelin brothers came up with the idea as a way to advertise their tyres. You will probably hear the word Michelin used in relation to both restaurants and cars, a strange combination, but it makes sense when you understand the background.

In 1898 the Michelin brothers opened a tyre factory in Clermont-Ferrand in central France, which was to become the largest such factory in the world. The pneumatic tyre (air-filled) was still being developed and the Michelin brothers invented the radial tyre which is made by most tyre manufacturers today. Recognizing the link between travel and the need for good travel guides, which would give a newcomer to an area an idea of what they could expect to find, the Michelin brothers introduced the first Michelin guide book in 1900. The star ratings given to the restaurants by the guide have now become the most famous and sought-after in the world. Chefs at the top restaurants are under tremendous pressure not to lose a star once they have gained a Michelin rating.

Entente Cordiale

In April 2004 Queen Elizabeth II went to France to meet with the French prime minister to celebrate the centenary of the Entente Cordiale. The Entente Cordiale, which means 'friendly understanding', was an agreement drawn up and signed by France and Britain on 4 April 1904, which declared that each country recognized the other's world interests and agreed not to obstruct the other in the pursuit of them.

It was very important historically as France and Britain have, for all their very close links over the centuries, been in competition with each other, particularly in terms of claiming territories. This had resulted in a seemingly endless round of conflicts. The growth of the German navy during the early 1900s gave Britain cause for concern and France became the natural ally against the potential threat. Thus for the last hundred years France and Britain have had 'a special agreement' which was initially the basis for the alliance of the two countries against Germany during the First World War.

Concorde

You will have heard of Concorde, the fastest plane in the world, that travelled so fast it broke the sound barrier.

What you may not realise is that the first Concorde to fly was the prototype Concorde 001, built by the French. The project began as a joint project between Britain and France to develop a supersonic aircraft, and they signed a draft treaty to that effect in November 1962. Concorde 001 first flew from Toulouse airport in March 1969, and the British prototype Concorde 002 flew from Filton in April of that year.

Concorde was able to cross the Atlantic so quickly that in 1985 Phil Collins used it to perform two concerts in the same day, one in America, one in Britain, for the charity Live Aid. The fastest crossing was 2hrs 52 mins 59 secs. Concorde was capable of travelling at twice the speed of sound, which is about the speed that a bullet leaves a gun.

Concorde made its last flight in October 2003, flying at up to 1,350 mph, across the Atlantic Ocean. Having been the first to fly them, Air France was the first to retire their Concorde planes, doing so in May 2003.

Astérix

The comic adventures of Astérix and his bunch of friends are very popular and have been translated into many languages and become known all over the world. You may have seen the TV cartoon version of these stories, but Astérix started out in the 1950s as a series of comics, created in France by writer René Goscinny and artist Albert Uderzo. Set in the year 50BC, the stories tell of the exploits of a plucky bunch of Gauls who are in constant conflict with the Romans, and who have the advantage of being able to use Druid magic to fool their enemies. They are still loved by people of all ages today. There was even a movie version of the stories made in 2001.

Babar

The delightful children's books about Babar the Elephant are to the French what Winnie the Pooh is to the British. Babar educated other elephants in human ways, and built a town named Celesteville after his wife, Celeste. Written and illustrated by French author Jean de Brunhoff, the first book in the series was published in 1931 and was a version of a bedtime story that Jean's wife used to tell to their son, Laurent, when he was a child. After his father died, Laurent carried on writing Babar stories, which had become hugely popular and were read to, and by, children all over the world.

Christian Dior

Christian Dior was born in Normandy in 1905. From an early age he showed great talent as an artist, and in 1935 moved to Paris to sell his fashion sketches. He became more and more interested in fashion, and in 1946

managed to open his own fashion house. In 1947 Christian Dior suddenly became a worldwide name, when his 'New Look' was launched. It doesn't sound possible that a set of dress designs could cause so much interest and news, but, a bit like Coco Chanel, Dior was doing something different. He was bringing a very modern, and luxurious, style of fashion to women who had lived through the deprivation of the Second World War.

During wartime, people in countries such as Britain and France had to accept the fact that the most important thing the governments had to spend money on was weapons and soldiers. As a result clothes were considered less important, and fashions became very unexciting. Well, it makes sense. If a country could only produce a limited amount of silk, then it was better to use it to make parachutes that could save airmen's lives, than to make lovely silk dresses that couldn't. The most important thing for a designer to think of, during the War, was how to make as many clothes as possible out of as little fabric as possible, which was a bit boring. Then, after the War, Christian Dior showed his new designs which used lots of fabric in swishy, pretty skirts, and clothes were exciting again.

Unfortunately, most people were still recovering from the hardship of wartime, in Britain food and clothes were still being rationed (rationing meant that everybody had a list of things they were allowed to buy each week, and coupons from the government to ensure they weren't allowed to buy any more than was on the list).

So, when Christian Dior showed his dresses, some of which needed more than ten metres of fabric to make them, he caused a scandal. People became very angry, and felt that his designs were encouraging people to be very wasteful, people as far away as America protested against the designs. Some people called his clothes 'The Revolution', and models wearing his clothes even had them torn off them! (That makes the beginnings of Punk, that was meant to be so shocking, sound a bit dull in comparison.)

But eventually the fuss died down, Dior remained popular and each of his following fashion shows was a huge success.

Emergency Phrases

Greetings

hello	*bonjour*
hi/see you	*salut*
yes	*oui*
no	*non*
good evening	*bonsoir*
thank you	*merci*
goodbye	*au revoir*
see you later	*à bientôt*
please	*s'il vous plaît*
okay	*d'accord*

Getting around

exit	*sortie*
right	*droite*
left	*gauche*
no entry	*entrée interdite*
Where are the toilets?	*Où sont les toilettes?*
I'm lost	*Je suis perdu* (if you are a boy; if you are a girl it's spelt *perdue* but is pronounced the same way)
Can you help me please?	*Vous pouvez m'aider,* *s'il vous plaît?*
Where is (the shop)?	*Où est (le magasin)?*
Where are (the shops)?	*Où sont (les magasins)?*
Go straight ahead	*Allez tout droit*
Can you draw me a map?	*Vous pouvez me dessiner un plan?*

About you

I am English/American/Irish/Scottish/Welsh (for boys)	*Je suis anglais/américain/irlandais/écossais/gallois*
I am English/American/Irish/Scottish/Welsh (for girls)	*Je suis anglaise/américaine/irlandaise/écossaise/galloise*
I'm on holiday	*Je suis en vacances*
I don't understand	*Je ne comprends pas*
Can you repeat that?	*Vous pouvez répéter?*
Do you speak English?	*Vous parlez anglais?*
I'm cold	*J'ai froid*
I'm hot	*J'ai chaud*
I am eight	*J'ai huit ans*
I am nine	*J'ai neuf ans*
I am ten	*J'ai dix ans*
My name is	*Je m'appelle*

Eating

I like	*J'aime*
I love	*J'adore*
I don't like	*Je n'aime pas*
I'm hungry	*J'ai faim*
I'm thirsty	*J'ai soif*
I am a vegetarian (if you are a boy)	*Je suis végétarien*
I am a vegetarian (if you are a girl)	*Je suis végétarienne*

Food

chocolate	*le chocolat*
chocolate croissant	*le pain au chocolat*
crisps	*les chips*

chips	*les frites*
pizza	*la pizza*
bread	*le pain*
salt	*le sel*
butter	*le beurre*
hot chocolate	*le chocolat chaud*
fruit juice	*le jus de fruit*
coke	*le coca*
milk shake	*le milk-shake*
milk	*le lait*
squeezed lemon to which you add your own sugar (*sucre*) and water	*le citron pressé*
water	*l'eau*
fizzy water	*l'eau gazeuse*
still water	*l'eau plate*
Can I have the bill please?	*L'addition, s'il vous plaît*

Meals

breakfast	*le petit déjeuner*
lunch	*le déjeuner*
evening meal, dinner	*le dîner*
starter	*un hors-d'œuvres*
second course	*l'entrée*
main course	*le plat principal*
cheese course	*le plateau de fromage*
dessert	*le dessert*
ice cream	*une glace*

Cutlery

plate	*une assiette*
knife	*un couteau*
fork	*une fourchette*
spoon	*une cuillère*
glass	*un verre*

Things to do

to watch telly	*regarder la télé*
to play football	*jouer au football*
to read	*lire*
to swim	*nager*
swimming pool	*la piscine*
to listen to music	*écouter de la musique*
to dance	*danser*

Shopping

I would like	*Je voudrais*
How much is it?	*C'est combien?*
this one	*celui-ci*
I would like to buy	*Je voudrais acheter*
I'll take it	*Je le prends*
too expensive	*trop cher*

Shops

grocer	*une épicerie*
butcher	*une boucherie*
baker	*une boulangerie*

chemist	une pharmacie
cake shop	une pâtisserie
shopping centre	un centre commercial
post office	la poste

Other phrases

I am ill	Je suis malade
It hurts	Ça fait mal
I'm full	Je n'ai plus faim
I don't like dancing	Je n'aime pas danser
Have you got Playstation™?	Est-ce que tu as une Playstation™?
Whose go is it?	C'est à qui?
It's my turn	C'est à moi
Great!	Super!
Cool	Cool
Very cool	Trop cool
So cool it's hot!	C'est d'enfer
Shut up	Tais-toi!
I am a fan of …	Je suis fan de…
Can I play with you?	Est-ce que je peux jouer avec toi?
Are you on the Internet?	Est-ce que tu as Internet?
Harry Potter	Harry Potter
The Hobbit	Bilbo le Hobbit
The Lord of the Rings	Le Seigneur des Anneaux
I'm bored	Je m'ennuie
	(Hopefully you won't need this!)

Good Books

Asterix and Obelix all at Sea
Asterix and Son
Albert Uderzo
(Orion Paperback, 2001, 2002)
Two of the many Asterix adventures. You can also read these in the original French.

Tintin in Tibet
The Calculus Affair
Hergé
(Mammoth Paperback, 2002)
Belgian rather than French, but widely read in France (even by adults). Also available in French, and there are many more in the series.

The Stormin' Normans
Terry Deary
(Scholastic, 2001)
One of the Horrible Histories series, looking at our distant French ancestors.

The Frightful First World War and the Woeful Second World War
Terry Deary
(Scholastic, 2003)
The Horrible Histories of the two world wars.

The Count of Monte Cristo
Alexandre Dumas
(Puffin Classics, 1996)
Shortened version of a classic tale.

The Three Musketeers
Alexandre Dumas
(Puffin Classics, 1986)
Another famous story by Dumas, in a shortened version.

A Tale of Two Cities
Charles Dickens
(Puffin Classics, 1995)

The Scarlet Pimpernel
Baroness Orczy
(Puffin Classics, 1997)

Biggles in France
Captain W.E. Johns
(Red Fox, 1993)

Perrault's Fairy Tales
Charles Perrault
(Houghton Mifflin, 1993)

Impressionist Art
Off the Wall Museum Guides
for Kids
Ruthie Knapp; Janice
Lehmberg
(Davis Publications, 1998)

Out of Darkness
The Story of Louis Braille
Russell Freedman
(Houghton Mifflin, 1997)

Joan of Arc
Michael Morpurgo
(Chrysalis Books, 1998)

France for Dummies
Darwin Porter, Danforth
Prince, Cheryl A. Pientka
(Wiley, 2003)

The French Confection
Anthony Horowitz
(Walker Books Paperback,
2003)
A children's thriller,
featuring the Diamond
brothers, set in Paris.

French language books
Encore Tricolore
Sylvia Honnor, Heather
Mascie-Taylor (Editor)
(Nelson Thornes, 2001)

Charlie et la Chocolaterie
Roald Dahl
(Gallimard-Jeunesse
Paperback, 2002)
This is *Charlie and the
Chocolate Factory* translated
into French.

Usborne Easy French
K. Daynes, N. Irving
(Usborne Paperback 2002)

*Usborne French Dictionary for
Beginners*
(Usborne Paperback 2002)

*The Usborne Picture
Dictionary in French*
Felicity Brooks
(Usborne Paperback 2003)

Wicked Websites

www.franceway.com
All about what to do and where to go.

www.disneylandparis.com
The official Disneyland Paris site.

www.francetourism.com
The site for the French government tourist office, with some nice pics of France.

www.mappy.fr
How to get around by car, how far each place is from another. Work out how far you are going.

www.parisdigest.com
Good photos and info on Paris.

www.usborne-quicklinks.com
Lots of useful stuff on the French language, including pronunciations

www.louvre.fr
The Louvre in Paris, one of the world's greatest museums.

www.mae.org
The Musée de l'Air et de l'Espace – the oldest flight and aircraft museum in the world, just outside Paris.

www.parcasterix.fr
Parc Astérix, which includes one of the best roller coasters in Europe.

www.chateauversailles.fr
The amazing Château de Versailles , Louis XIV's palace and gardens, just outside Paris.